Overcoming Worldliness

by Heath Rogers

© 2020 One Stone Press.
All rights reserved. No part of this book may be reproduced in any form without written permission of the publisher.

Published by:
One Stone Press
979 Lovers Lane
Bowling Green, KY 42103

Printed in the United States of America

ISBN: 978-1-941422-54-0

www.onestone.com

Table of Contents

Lesson 1: The Christian and the World 7

Lesson 2: Drugs and Alcohol 13

Lesson 3: Fornication 21

Lesson 4: Homosexuality 29

Lesson 5: Involvement in Pornography 37

Lesson 6: Dancing 47

Lesson 7: Immodesty - Part 1 55

Lesson 8: Immodesty - Part 2 63

Lesson 9: Gambling 71

Lesson 10: Materialism 77

Lesson 11: Sinful Speech 85

Lesson 12: Hatred 93

Lesson 13: A Bad Reputation 101

Dedication

This book is dedicated to Mike and Jan Hepner. Their faithful service to the Lord, constant encouragement to God's people, and unwavering support of gospel preaching have made them dear friends and great examples to everyone who knows them.

Introduction

Years ago, an elder in the church told me that an older preacher had told him that worldliness was the greatest threat facing the Lord's church. Things have not changed.

Just as church members, because of where they walk, bring dirt into the church building on the bottoms of their shoes, so also, because of how some members choose to live, they bring the world into the church. Converts often come into the Lord's church without fully abandoning their worldly ways. Some who are raised in the church long to enjoy the sinful pleasures of the world around them. Some elders turn blind eyes; some preachers speak in generalities without making specific applications; and the sin in the church worsens.

When we hear a Christian say, "I don't see anything wrong with dancing, drinking in moderation, playing the lottery, or wearing revealing clothing," we know that person's moral compass is aligned with the world, not with Scripture. However, these days we also hear, "I see nothing wrong with getting a tattoo;" "we shouldn't be so condemning of homosexuals;" or "I caught my husband viewing pornography!" Today's church is suffering through the drug epidemic that is impacting the world around us. Adultery is common, even among preachers, elders, and deacons. Divorce among brethren occurs at an alarming rate. Through their social media posts, Christians often reflect a love for the world. No, things have not changed. Satan is still having his way with many of God's people.

The Bible still says, "Come out from among them and be separate, says the Lord. Do not touch what is unclean, and I will receive you. I will be a Father to you, and you shall be My sons and daughters, says the Lord Almighty" (2 Corinthians 6:17-18). God said, "Be holy, for I am holy" (1 Peter 1:16). His standards have not changed. It is time for today's Christians to take the worldliness that is permeating the Lord's church seriously.

In this workbook, we consider numerous forms of worldliness that trouble God's people. The lessons look at how these various practices violate the standards God has clearly set forth in His word, and then consider what we can do to overcome these challenges in our lives. The final lesson addresses the importance of maintaining our influence and reputations in this world.

I am extremely grateful to Carolyn Bixby for taking the time to proofread this material. Many of her suggestions are a part of this workbook.

Unless otherwise noted, all Bible quotations are taken from the New King James Version.

The Christian and the World

Lesson 1

"Therefore 'Come out from among them and be separate, says the Lord. Do not touch what is unclean, and I will receive you. I will be a Father to you, and you shall be My sons and daughters, says the Lord Almighty'" (2 Corinthians 6:17-18).

God's people now, as always, face the challenge of living in the world without being part of it. The church constantly battles different forms of worldliness because its members struggle to separate themselves from the world and the uncleanliness that surrounds them.

Christians are to be holy

God does not call us to live carelessly in this world. "But as He who called you is holy, you also be holy in all your conduct, because it is written, 'Be holy, for I am holy'" (1 Peter 1:15-16).

> ...it is written, "Be **holy**, for I am holy."
> - 1 Peter 1:16

The concept of holiness is set forth very well in the Old Testament, especially in the book of Leviticus, from which Peter quoted in the above passage. The priesthood, the tabernacle, and its furnishings, were set apart for service to God.

In the New Testament, the word "holy" emphasizes a moral or ethical separation from the world's filth. The Greek word *hagios* means "set apart for God, to be, as it were, exclusively his" but, "in a moral sense, pure, sinless, upright, holy" (Thayer 7). Being holy means being separate from the world's sin and consecrated to God for His use and His glory.

While this separation takes place when we are saved and, through baptism, washed from our sins, we must also participate in a continuing, purposeful separation from the sins of the world. After telling the Corinthians they must come out from among the sin around them and not touch what is unclean, Paul wrote, "Therefore, having these promises, beloved, let us cleanse ourselves from all filthiness of the flesh and spirit, perfecting holiness in the fear of God" (2 Corinthians 7:1). We must cleanse ourselves from the filthy habits, attitudes, values, and influences in our lives. To perfect holiness is to bring to completion God's desire for us to be holy. Christians are obligated to live holy lives. This means we must, to the best of our ability, be pure and upright.

When the Lord returns, we are to be found "blameless in holiness before our God" (1 Thessalonians 3:13). This does not happen automatically when one becomes a Christian. It is the end result of a life lived with purpose and determination to rid oneself from sin and pursue the standards set forth in God's word (Romans 12:2). It would be nice if we could do this in a perfect environment free from temptation to do wrong, but Christians are challenged to live holy lives in an unholy world.

The world

The Bible uses the word "world" in different ways. Sometimes, it refers to the physical earth (Acts 17:24; Mark 16:15); and sometimes, it refers to the earth's inhabitants (John 3:16; 1 Corinthians 4:9).

The Bible also uses the word "world" to refer to the sinful things in this realm, things that oppose God's holiness and tempt us to sin. "For all that is in the world—the lust of the flesh, the lust of the eyes, and the pride of life—is not of the Father but is of the world" (1 John 2:16). The world is the source of moral and spiritual "corruption" (2 Peter 1:4) and "pollutions" (2:20). It contains the evil dispositions and aims of sinful men, the immoral tendencies and pursuits that oppose God, His word, and His ways.

These things exist because "the world lies under the sway of the wicked one" (1 John 5:19), who is

> We know that we are of **God**, and the whole **world** lies under the **sway** of the **wicked** one.
> - 1 John 5:19

"the ruler of this world" (John 14:30). God and this sinful world are diametrically opposed to each other. Christians must choose between the two. We cannot serve two masters (Matthew 6:24). "Adulterers and adulteresses! Do you not know that friendship with the world is enmity with God? Whoever therefore wants to be a friend of the world makes himself an enemy of God" (James 4:4; c.f. 1 John 2:15).

Instead of searching for a place in this sinful world, we must observe and conduct ourselves as sojourners and pilgrims here (1 Peter 2:11). A sojourner is one who is lives in a country temporarily, without permanent or official residency. We are not citizens of the world, and we have no claim to any property. For this reason, we can sing, "This world is not my home, I'm just a passing thru." If we are Christians, our citizenship is in Heaven (Philippians 3:20). This world hates us, and it shows this hatred in various ways; but our faith (demonstrated by active obedience) gives us victory over this world and its hatred (1 John 5:4). Our faith must move us to walk in this world while responding to temptations in the proper manner.

The Christian and the sinful things of the world

Regarding the sinful things of the world, the Christian finds himself in one of three possible situations—he remains innocent; he gets involved; or he is victorious. To live holy lives, we must respond to each situation appropriately.

1. **If you are innocent of a specific sin, continue to avoid it.** If you have never been involved in a specific sin, you are in the best possible situation, and God's word exhorts you to avoid and abstain from it.

    The word "abstain" means to voluntarily hold oneself back or away from something. God does not put up guard rails along the highways

> For whatever is born of **God** overcomes the **world**. And this is the **victory** that has overcome the world— our **faith**.
>
> - 1 John 5:4

> Beloved, I beg you as **sojourners** and **pilgrims**, abstain from **fleshly lusts** which war against the **soul**.
>
> - 1 Peter 2:11

we travel through in this dangerous world. He respects our free will and allows us to go wherever we wish. To live holy lives, we must voluntarily hold ourselves back from "fleshly lusts which war against the soul" (1 Peter 2:11). We are to test all things according to the standard set forth in God's word, clinging to what is good and abstaining from every form of evil (1 Thessalonians 5:22-23).

Solomon wrote the book of Proverbs to warn his sons to avoid the pitfalls of life (Proverbs 3:21-23; 4:14-15). He wanted to spare them the consequences of traveling down sin's pathways. If you have not committed a specific sin, don't do it! You save yourself the struggle of the following two steps.

2. **If you are currently involved in a sin, you must overcome it.** Sin seeks to capture and ensnare. Fleshly lusts war against the soul. You must win these battles.

Jesus exhorted all seven churches of Asia to overcome (Revelation 2:7, 11, 17, 26; 3:5, 12, 21). The word "overcome" is translated from the Greek word *nakaoo* which means, "to conquer; to carry off the victory, come off victorious... used of one who by Christian constancy and courage keeps himself unharmed and spotless from his adversary's devices, solicitations, assaults" (Thayer 425-426). We do not overcome by surrendering. We overcome when we subdue and conquer the sin in our lives.

In order to overcome a sin, one must truly repent and turn away from it. "Repent therefore of this your wickedness, and pray God if perhaps the thought of your heart may be forgiven you. For I see that you are poisoned by bitterness and bound by iniquity" (Acts 8:22-23).

We must remember that, while we are in this world, we are in enemy territory. It is important that we put on the whole armor of God so we can withstand the devil's attacks (Ephesians 6:10-17).

3. If you have overcome a sin, you must not go back to that sin.
Once you conquer and escape a specific sin, stay away from it! There is a danger of becoming entangled in that sin again (2 Peter 2:20).

We must keep ourselves unspotted from the world (James 1:27). Now that we are Christians, we must not return to our former lusts; we must be holy in all our conduct (1 Peter 1:14-16). Cease from sin; walk according to God's will; do not pursue worldly lusts (1 Peter 4:1-4).

God's grace does not give us license to sin (Romans 6:1-2, 15). It teaches us to practice self-control (Titus 2:11-12). Too many Christians have relaxed attitudes towards worldly lusts. This is why worldliness is such a problem among God's people. We are admonished to keep ourselves separate from the lusts of the world as we perfect holiness in our lives.

Conclusion

Christians live as sojourners in this world of sinful lusts that war against our souls. Maintaining a proper relationship with the world is essential to maintaining fellowship with God. We must come out from the world and be separate, not touching what is unclean, and God will receive us as His people (2 Corinthians 6:17-18).

Spiritual dangers abound in this world. We are in enemy territory. Its sinful pleasures are not ours to enjoy. Instead, we ought to live holy lives that reflect God's holiness.

In the remaining lessons in this book, we will study some specific areas of worldliness and consider ways to avoid and overcome them.

Questions

1. What challenge has God's people always experienced in this world (2 Corinthians 6:17-18)? _____

2. What does the word "holy" mean? _____

Overcoming Worldliness

3. What does it mean to "perfect holiness" (2 Corinthians 7:1)? _____

4. Is perfecting holiness something God does to us, or something in which we must participate? _____

5. Why is the world opposed to God (1 John 5:19)? _____

6. Explain why trying to be a friend of the world makes one an enemy of God (James 4:4). _____

7. How are Christians to see and conduct themselves in this world (1 Peter 2:11)? _____

8. Explain why it is best to be innocent of sin, to have never committed a specific sin in the first place. _____

9. What does the word "abstain" mean? _____

10. The word "overcome" is translated from the Greek word *nakaoo*. What does this word mean? _____

11. What actions are necessary if we are to overcome sin (Acts 8:22-23; Ephesians 6:10-17)? _____

12. What does God's grace teach us (Titus 2:11-12)? _____

Drugs and Alcohol

Drugs and alcohol have caused problems in our society for a long time. They are a part of the world in which we live and affect our lives in many different ways. Despite warnings and education, there is no indication that the problems caused by drugs and alcohol are going to be solved any time soon.

The problems associated with drugs and alcohol can be approached from several different directions. Others are more qualified to talk about the health concerns and the impact drugs and alcohol have on our society. This lesson addresses the use of drugs, alcohol, and tobacco from a Biblical perspective.

The Bible condemns drug and alcohol use as works of the flesh

The consumption of alcohol causes drunkenness, which Paul identified as a work of the flesh (Galatians 5:19-21). Drunkenness is a state of intoxication. Christians understand that drunkenness is a sin; yet, we sometimes hear the question, "Is it all right for a Christian to consume alcohol as long as he does not get drunk?"

Various degrees of alcohol consumption are condemned in 1 Peter 4:3. "For we have spent enough of our past lifetime in doing the will of the Gentiles—when we walked in lewdness, lusts, **drunkenness, revelries, drinking parties**, and abominable idolatries" (emphasis mine, HR).

Revelries is translated from the Greek word *komos*, which is defined as "a nocturnal and riotous procession of half-drunken and frolicsome fellows who after supper parade through the streets with torches and music in honor of Bacchus or some

> Now the **works of the flesh** are evident... **drunkenness**, revelries, and the like... those who practice such things **will not inherit** the kingdom of God.
> - Galatians 5:19-21

other deity, and sing and play before the house of their male and female friends; hence used generally, of feasts and drinking-parties that are protracted till late at night and indulge in revelry" (Thayer 367).

Brother Clinton Hamilton made the following comment regarding *komos*: "It refers to boisterous noise making conduct or carousals that are uninhibited because of the profligate behavior arising either from their uncontrolled passions or minds disabled by strong drink" (Hamilton 214). This word includes, and condemns, modern-day keg parties and wild house parties. Such are sinful. No Christian has any business attending such parties, whether he is drinking alcohol or not.

Drinking parties is translated from the Greek word *potos* which refers to a drinking party that does not involve drunkenness. This includes, and condemns, social drinking. "The cocktail parties characteristic of some segments of contemporary society fit perfectly in this classification for they are drinking parties when there is an imbibing of alcoholic beverages which take away the moral restraints and good judgment of those who participate in the drinking. Unrestrained, their conduct devolves into carousing" (Hamilton 214-215).

> **Abstain** from every **form** of **evil**.
> - 1 Thessalonians 5:22

The social drinker is not abstaining from every form of evil (1 Thessalonians 5:22). He is setting a terrible example and is a potential stumbling block to a young or weak Christian (Matthew 18:6-7).

The works of the flesh also include the sin of sorcery (Galatians 5:20). While we may not readily associate sorcery with drug and alcohol use, the original Greek language makes this connection very clear. Sorcery is translated from the Greek word *pharmakeia* from which we get our English word pharmacy. This word "primarily signified 'the use of medicine, drugs, spells'; then, 'poisoning'; then, 'sorcery'... In 'sorcery,' the use of drugs, whether simple or potent, was generally accompanied by incantations and appeals to occult powers, with the provision of various charms, amulets, etc., professedly designed to keep the applicant or patient from the attention and power of demons, but actually to impress the applicant with the mysterious resources and powers of the sorcerer'" (Vine's 587). Thus, we see that the use of mind-altering drugs is condemned as a work of the flesh.

Drugs and alcohol impair sobriety and self-control

The Scriptures call upon God's people to be sober. "Therefore gird up the loins of your mind, be sober, and rest your hope fully upon the grace that is to be brought to you at the revelation of Jesus Christ" (1 Peter 1:13; cf. 1 Thessalonians 5:6-8). The word sober is translated from the Greek word *nepho* which means, "to be free from the influence of intoxicants" (Vine's 583). We are to be in control of our minds and passions. Alcohol impairs sound judgment (Isaiah 28:7), but how much alcohol does it take to impair one's judgment? When does a person come under the influence of intoxicants? It takes only one drink.

"Alcohol is metabolized extremely quickly by the body. Unlike foods, which require time for digestion, alcohol needs no digestion and is quickly absorbed. Alcohol gets 'VIP' treatment in the body—absorbing and metabolizing before most other nutrients. About 20 percent is absorbed directly across the walls of an empty stomach and can reach the brain within one minute" (www.healthchecksystems.com/alcohol.htm).

Any Bible passage that commands soberness and self-control condemns the recreational use of drugs and alcohol.

Drugs and alcohol are addictive

"All things are lawful for me, but all things are not helpful. All things are lawful for me, but I will not

> But let us who are of the **day** be **sober**, putting on the breastplate of **faith** and **love**, and as a helmet the **hope** of **salvation**.
>
> - 1 Thessalonians 5:8

Ongoing use demands increased use

Drugs are chemicals which affect the pleasure centers of the human brain. They mimic biological chemicals that our bodies produce naturally to create pleasure. The recreation of this pleasure is the "high" that drug users experience. The problem is that the human body builds up a tolerance to these artificial chemicals, and more of them are needed to produce the same sensation.

Drug users will sometimes increase their usage, move on to more potent drugs, or combine drugs in their effort to experience the same "high." These increases and experiments are dangerous and sometimes deadly.

be brought under the power of any" (1 Corinthians 6:12). Christians are not to allow themselves to be "brought under the power of," "mastered by" (NASU), or "enslaved by" (ESV) anything.

Christians should avoid drugs and alcohol because drugs and alcohol are addictive. They have the power to enslave their users (Hosea 4:11). Some prescription drugs are highly addictive. Tobacco contains nicotine, which is very addictive.

An addict's life is very hard. He struggles daily to fight strong urges and impulses to feed his addiction. It is an incredible cross to bear. Why would a Christian take a chance and expose himself to a substance already proven to be addictive? No Christian would have to struggle as an alcoholic, drug addict, or smoker if he avoided taking the first drink, hit, drag, etc.

Drugs and alcohol destroy the body

Your physical body is not your own to do with as you please. "Or do you not know that your body is the temple of the Holy Spirit who is in you, whom you have from God, and you are not your own? For you were bought at a price; therefore glorify God in your body and in your spirit, which are God's" (1 Corinthians 6:19-20). Your body belongs to God. Willingly doing something that could destroy the body is a sin. Drugs, alcohol, and tobacco have been proven to damage the body and destroy health.

Drugs and alcohol are illegal

Christians must obey the laws of the land (Romans 13:1-2). Not all drugs are illegal. Alcohol and tobacco can be purchased legally and used by those who meet the age requirements. A growing number of states have legalized marijuana. Some narcotics can be purchased and used with a doctor's prescription. However, it is against the law to buy, sell, possess, and use many of the drugs under consideration in this lesson.

Drugs and alcohol use brings misery and loss

TV shows, movies, and songs often depict alcohol in a positive light. Beer commercials can be humorous and portray the consumption of beer as innocent and enjoyable.

The Bible pulls no punches in setting forth the pitiful plight of those who are addicted to alcohol. Read Proverbs 23:29-35 very carefully.

Not only do drugs and alcohol destroy the lives of their users, but they also bring misery upon others. Spouses and children are neglected or abused. Parents of alcoholics and drug addicts undergo emotional turmoil, and sometimes physical harm and the loss of their possessions. Innocent people are often maimed or killed by drunk drivers. Society endures the crime and financial burdens associated with drug and alcohol addiction.

A Christian cannot willingly, and in good conscience, partake of something that causes so much destruction to others. Those who purchase alcohol support a multi-billion-dollar industry that contributes to pain and misery suffered by many people. Such violates the Golden Rule and Second Greatest Commandment (Matthew 7:12; 22:39). We are to have no fellowship with the works of darkness (Ephesians 5:11). We are to abstain from every form of evil (1 Thessalonians 5:22).

Why some people try drugs, alcohol and tobacco

Despite the passing and enforcement of laws, warnings, and continued education, young people still try, and become addicted to, drugs, alcohol, and tobacco. Christians need to understand that the Bible provides an answer for any reason one might use to justify trying drugs, alcohol, and tobacco.

Some try drugs, alcohol, or tobacco because of peer pressure. Everyone else appears to be doing

> And have no **fellowship** with the **unfruitful** works of **darkness**, but rather **expose** them.
> - Ephesians 5:11

it. They think it is strange that we aren't (1 Peter 4:4). Christians are to be leaders, not followers. We are not to conform to the world and do the things the world wants us to do (Romans 12:2).

For some people, drinking alcohol or trying drugs is a rite of passage into adulthood, or a means of proving their maturity. There can be dire consequences to proving we can live like the world lives (Galatians 6:7-8). The Bible warns us to abstain from things such as drugs and alcohol so we can live free from these consequences.

Some people drink and use drugs to escape reality. They do not want to face life's hardships, so they seek the temporary escape offered by drugs and alcohol. The Bible does not allow us to escape reality; rather, God gives us everything we need to face and endure whatever lies before us (Philippians 4:6-7; Hebrew 4:16; 2 Peter 1:3).

Some people drink and use drugs for pleasure. The world's pleasures are both fleeting and dying (Hebrews 11:25; 1 John 2:15-17). We are to rejoice in the Lord, not in a bottle, needle, pill, or joint.

Christians have no business trying drugs, alcohol, or tobacco. It is not worth the risk of becoming addicted, harming yourself, or bringing sorrow to others.

Conclusion

Under the Old Law, both the priests and the kings were forbidden to drink alcohol (Leviticus 10:9-10; Proverbs 31:4-5). They needed sound minds as they served the Lord. Christians are both priests and kings (1 Peter 2:5, 9; Revelation 1:3). We are called to serve the Lord with sobriety and sound judgment. We are not to be drunk with wine, but filled with the Spirit (Ephesians 5:18).

Advances in technology will provide new drugs and new ways to use them. Laws will likely continue to change, further legalizing the use of some of these drugs. However, none of these things changes the truth set forth in the Bible. We need to know what the Bible says about drug, alcohol, and tobacco use, understand the principles such behavior violates, and stand behind them.

Questions

1. Describe the degrees of alcohol consumption that are condemned in 1 Peter 4:3. _____
   _____
   _____

LESSON 2 Drugs and Alcohol   19

2. Explain why the word sorcery or witchcraft in Galatians 5:20 includes, and thus condemns, the use of mind-altering drugs. _____
_____
_____

3. What does the consumption of alcohol do to one's judgment (Isaiah 28:7)?
_____
_____

4. How much alcohol must a person consume before he comes under its intoxicating influence? _____
_____

5. What does alcohol do to one's heart (mind) (Hosea 4:11)? _____
_____
_____

6. To whom does your physical body belong (1 Corinthians 6:19-20)?_____
_____

7. How does Proverbs 23:29-35 describe the person who is addicted to alcohol? _____
_____
_____

8. What admonition is given in Proverbs 23:31?_____
_____
_____

9. What can we expect from the world if we choose to abstain from drugs, alcohol, and tobacco (1 Peter 4:4)? _____
_____
_____

10. Some people use drugs and alcohol to escape the hardships of life. Is this an option for the Christian? Explain why or why not. _____
_____
_____
_____

20 Overcoming Worldliness

Lesson 3

Fornication

The numerous New Testament admonitions against the sin of fornication appear to be custom-made for our generation. Our culture is saturated with sexually oriented images and messages. We are constantly bombarded by advertisements, billboard signs, and magazine covers featuring half-naked people selling everything from auto parts to shampoo. Sex is a primary ingredient in all entertainment forms—movies, TV programs, songs, and books. This appears to reflect the attitudes of those around us. Adultery, random hookups, teen pregnancy, and illicit cohabitation are unfortunate fixtures in our society.

It may be hard to believe, but this sin was even more prevalent in the first century. "A feature of life in a Greek city of the first century was its laxity in matters of sexual morality" (Morris 23). Restraint from fulfilling sexual desires was regarded as an unreasonable demand to place upon individuals. It was common for married men to have mistresses, concubines, and female slaves to fulfill their sexual appetites.

Prostitution abounded throughout the Roman Empire. It was often connected with the worship at the various idol temples. "Many of the rites of pagan worship were extremely coarse and sensual, thereby lending to immorality the sanction of religion. In the worship of Aphrodite at Corinth a thousand priestesses devoted themselves to prostitution in the name of religion. There has been found in Antioch of Pisidia remains of a 'holy bed' which was used for the mystic marriage ceremony between the god and his goddess—in which service, according to immemorial traditions,

> Neither **fornicators**... nor **adulterers**... will inherit the **kingdom of God**.
> - 1 Corinthians 6:10

> Now the works of the **flesh** are evident, which are: **adultery, fornication, uncleanness, lewdness**... those who practice such things **will not inherit** the **kingdom of God**.
> - Galatians 5:19-21

Anatolian ladies, even of the highest rank, were expected to take part. A prominent feature of the worship of Artemis at Ephesus was the dedication to prostitution of a group of priestesses who came to the temple as chaste virgins. In Phrygia the worship of Cybele required of women in general that they sacrifice their virtue to the goddess, and if a husband should protest against his wife performing this service it was regarded as a grave offense, meriting the wrath of the goddess" (Dana 230).

The gospel first went out into this kind of a world. The chastity associated with Christianity was foreign to the Gentiles. Even after they were converted, the world constantly bombarded them to return to this sin. The epistles sent to the Gentile churches contain many admonitions against the sin of fornication. When sins are listed in these epistles, fornication is often mentioned first (1 Corinthians 6:9-10; Galatians 5:19-21; Ephesians 5:3-5; Colossians 3:5-7).

Satan has used the sin of fornication to weaken today's church. Our young people are bombarded with sexually oriented messages from many different sources. This fact, combined with peer pressure and hormones, makes the maintaining of their purity a mighty battle. Single adult Christians also struggle with these temptations; while married Christians must struggle to maintain purity in their marriages.

God's people have always needed to understand, live by, and uphold the Bible's teaching on fornication.

Fornication defined

The word "fornication" (sexual immorality in some translations) is from the Greek word *porneia*. Our English word porn comes from this Greek word, which is defined as "illicit sexual intercourse" (Thayer 532).

Fornication is actually an umbrella term that includes every kind of unlawful sexual activity (premarital sex, adultery, prostitution, homosexuality, incest, bestiality, etc.) that occurs prior to or outside of wedlock.

Christians sometime struggle with the temptation to get as close to fornication as they can without committing the sin. We need to understand that the Bible also condemns the sexual activity (petting, fondling, oral sex, etc.) that leads to intercourse. The words lewdness, lasciviousness, and sensuality are translated from the Greek word *aselgia*. This word is defined as "unbridled lust, excess, licentiousness, lasciviousness, wantonness, outrageousness, shamelessness, insolence... wanton acts or manners, as filthy words, indecent bodily movements, unchaste handling of males and females" (Thayer 79-80).

Why is fornication wrong?

Why is it wrong for two consenting adults to act on their natural desires?

1. **It is a sin against God.** When Potiphar's wife attempted to seduce Joseph, he replied, "How then can I do this great wickedness, and sin against God?" (Genesis 39:9). Joseph did not see fornication as the harmless fulfillment of a natural desire. He saw it as a violation of God's holiness and a transgression of His law.

   Sin is lawlessness or the transgression of the law (1 John 3:4). God has a law that governs the fulfillment of sexual desires. These desires are to be fulfilled in a lawful marriage relationship (1 Corinthians 7:1-5). Fornication disregards God's law, and it will always bring God's judgment and wrath (Hebrews 13:4; Colossians 3:5-6). The one who commits fornication will not inherit Heaven (1 Corinthians 6:9-10; Galatians 5:19-21; Ephesians 5:3-5).

2. **It is a sin against one's own body.** Fornication is a unique sin in that it violates and perverts

> Nevertheless, because of **sexual immorality**, let each man have his own **wife**, and let each woman have her own **husband**.
>
> - 1 Corinthians 7:2

> Therefore a man shall leave his father and mother and be **joined** to his wife, they shall become **one flesh**.
>
> - Genesis 2:24

God's plan and purpose for our physical bodies (1 Corinthians 6:13-20).

Despite having been converted to Christ, it appears that some members of the church in Corinth were still struggling with the sin of fornication. Remember, the temple of Aphrodite, with its 1,000 priestesses, was in Corinth. Paul reminded them that the act of fornication joins two physical bodies together in a special way. Sexual intimacy is a blessing God designed to bring husbands and wives together in the closest and most intimate of all possible human experiences—becoming one flesh (v. 16; Genesis 2:24).

Engaging in this act with someone other than one's own spouse is sinning against his own body. "Because sexual intimacy is the deepest uniting of two persons, its misuse corrupts on the deepest human level" (MacArthur 151). Not only are there spiritual consequences to fornication, there are also physical consequences (unplanned pregnancies and sexually transmitted diseases), as well as emotional consequences (loss of innocence, guilt, and shame).

3. **It is a sin against others.** Adultery, which falls under the umbrella term fornication, violates innocent people. Job saw adultery as a crime "to be punished by the judges" (Job 31:11, KJV, ESV). Solomon warned his sons about the severe consequences of committing adultery (Proverbs 6:30-35).

Adultery is a sin against society at large. It destroys marriages and homes, further decaying the moral fiber and foundation of our society. We all pay for the sin of adultery.

Premarital sex is a sin against another person. It is a form of theft. Paul wrote, "the wife does not have authority over her own body, but the husband does. And likewise the husband does not have authority over his own body, but the wife does" (1 Corinthians 7:4). Your body (your virginity) is not yours to give away to anyone you choose. It belongs to your spouse. Engaging in premarital sex takes that which belongs to your future spouse and gives it to another person who has no lawful right to it.

How to avoid fornication

Sexual desires are very strong, and opportunities to fulfill these desires abound in today's world. Following are some things we can do to help avoid the sin of fornication.

1. **Resolve not to sin against God.** Fornication is a sin, and God expects Christians to avoid all sin (1 John 2:1).

   Joseph faced a strong temptation regarding fornication (Genesis 39:7-9). His immediate response to this temptation was to refuse to commit the sin (v. 8). He identified fornication as a "great wickedness" and a "sin against God" (v. 9) and acted accordingly.

   There is physical pleasure in fornication, but as with all sin, the pleasure is only temporary (Hebrews 10:25). Afterward, there remains a price to pay (Proverbs 5:9-13; 6:24-29).

2. **Control your heart.** Sexual sins begin, and proceed from, the heart. "For out of the heart proceed evil thoughts, murders, adulteries, fornications, thefts, false witness, blasphemies" (Matthew 15:19). We must control our thoughts (Proverbs 4:23-27).

   "Looking at" leads to "lusting after" (Proverbs 6:25; 2 Samuel 11:2-4; Matthew 5:28). Sexual desires are often awakened and strengthened by the things we see. We can't always help what we see, but we can control what we stare at and meditate upon (Philippians 4:8).

> But I say to you that whoever **looks** at a woman to **lust** for her has already committed **adultery** with her in his **heart**.
>
> - Matthew 5:28

3. **Control your body.** Fornication may begin in the heart, but it is committed with the body. Despite the temptations that surround us, God expects us to maintain control over our bodies. "For this is the will of God, your sanctification: that you abstain from sexual immorality; that each one of you know how to control his own body in holiness and honor, not in the passion of lust like the Gentiles who do not know God" (1 Thessalonians 4:3-5, ESV).

   We are not to give in to sexual desires and temptations. We are to deny ungodliness and worldly lusts and live soberly, righteously, and godly in the present age (Titus 2:12). There are times when this requires an incredible amount of self-control, but God expects us to exercise such self-control.

4. **Do not put yourself in a position where you may be tempted.** "But put on the Lord Jesus Christ, and make no provision for the flesh, to fulfill its lusts" (Romans 13:14). It is foolish to place ourselves in temptation's path. Sometimes, Christians carelessly, or willingly, put themselves in the wrong places and among the wrong people (1 Corinthians 15:33; Proverbs 4:14-15). We are to avoid immoral people (Proverbs 5:3, 8; 7:10-23). We are to avoid things (dancing, immodest dress, movies with nudity or sexual content, etc.) that stimulate sexual interests and desires. We are to avoid situations (flirting, making-out, being alone with a member of the opposite sex, lowering our inhibitions through drug or alcohol use, etc.) that invite fornication.

5. **Flee fornication (1 Corinthians 6:18).** Flee is not a casual word. It is translated from the Greek word *pheugo*, which means to "flee away, seek safety by flight... to escape safe out of danger" (Thayer 651). This is how Joseph ultimately dealt with his temptation (Genesis 39:12). Some sins are overcome by fighting or resisting, but fornication is different. "When we are in danger of such immorality, we should not argue or debate or explain, and we certainly should not try to rationalize. We are not to consider it a spiritual challenge to be met but a spiritual trap to be escaped. We should get away as fast as we can" (MacArthur 151).

Conclusion

The Bible takes the sin of fornication very seriously. The world does not. Married people continue to commit adultery. Single adults and teens continue to engage in sexual sins. The teen pregnancy rate is still high, cohabitation rates are high, cases of sexually transmitted diseases are high. Sexual behavior is promoted, celebrated, and even aided by social media.

LESSON 3 Fornication 27

This is the world in which we are raising our young people. This is the world in which Christians are struggling to hold their marriages together and maintain sexual purity.

The battle is on, and we must win. God expects us to guard our hearts, to control our bodies, and to abstain from the sin of fornication.

Questions

1. In the New Testament the word fornication (sexual immorality) is translated from the Greek word *porneia*. Define this word. _____
   _____
   _____

2. Is sexual activity leading up to, but stopping short of, intercourse sinful? Why or why not? _____
   _____
   _____

3. What did Joseph say about the sin of fornication (Genesis 39:9)? _____
   _____
   _____

4. What did Job say about the sin of fornication (Job 31:11)?_____
   _____
   _____

5. According to 1 Corinthians 6:18, how is the sin of fornication different from every other sin?_____
   _____
   _____

6. Explain how adultery is a form of theft (Proverbs 6:30-35). _____
   _____
   _____

7. Explain how premarital sex is a form of theft (1 Corinthians 7:1-5). _____
   _____
   _____

8. What did Joseph finally have to do to avoid the sin of fornication (Genesis 39:12)?_____
   _____

Overcoming Worldliness

9. Define the word flee. _____
_____
_____

10. Where do sexual sins begin (Matthew 15:19; Proverbs 4:23)? _____
_____
_____

11. Where did David's sin with Bathsheba begin (2 Samuel 11:2-4)? _____
_____
_____

12. We are not to put ourselves in temptations (Romans 13:14). List some things we should avoid in order to maintain sexual purity. _____
_____
_____
_____
_____

Lesson 4

Homosexuality

There was a time when everyone understood homosexuality to be a sin. In our society, this time has long since passed. Since "coming out of the closet," the pro-homosexual agenda has made incredible strides. What we once condemned as an unacceptable perversion we now uphold as a harmless, alternate lifestyle. Those who sound forth to defend the Bible's teaching on this subject can, in some places, be accused of committing a hate crime and may even be prosecuted by the authorities, not to mention being condemned in the court of public opinion. It is a modern-day example of Isaiah 5:20. "Woe to those who call evil good, and good evil; who put darkness for light, and light for darkness; who put bitter for sweet, and sweet for bitter!"

Satan has made great strides in his efforts to bring this sin into the realm of religion. Some denominations, which used to oppose homosexuality as a sin, now accept homosexuals as members and ordain them as clergy. This sin has also impacted the Lord's church, even through the families of preachers, elders, and deacons. Satan is relentless in His efforts to destroy the influence of godly people.

God's people, young and old alike, are pressured to conform to the world's standards regarding homosexuality, same-sex marriage, and gender identity. In this lesson, we will take a simple and honest look at the Bible's teaching regarding these issues.

The Bible condemns homosexuality as a sin

Homosexual activity is identified and condemned as sinful in all three dispensations documented in the Bible.

> **Sodom and Gomorrah**... having given themselves over to **sexual immorality** and gone after **strange flesh**, are set forth as an example, suffering the **vengeance** of eternal fire.
>
> - Jude 7

During the **Patriarchal Age**, the destruction of Sodom and Gomorrah is a clear example of God's wrath against the sin of homosexuality.

When Lot chose to move to the plain of the Jordan, the men of Sodom were identified as being "exceedingly wicked and sinful against the Lord" (Genesis 13:13). As God moved forward to judge the cities, He told Abraham, "Because the outcry against Sodom and Gomorrah is great, and because their sin is very grave, I will go down now and see whether they have done altogether according to the outcry against it that has come to Me; and if not, I will know" (18:20-21). Abraham replied, "Will You also destroy the righteous with the wicked?" (v. 23).

Their wickedness was confirmed when the angels visited the city. "Now before they lay down, the men of the city, the men of Sodom, both old and young, all the people from every quarter, surrounded the house. And they called to Lot and said to him, 'Where are the men who came to you tonight? Bring them out to us that we may know them carnally'" (Genesis 19:4-5). The New Testament describes the sin of Sodom and Gomorrah as "having given themselves over to sexual immorality and gone after strange flesh" (Jude 7).

> "The degrading evil was so widespread that all of the men of Sodom, young and old alike, demanded that the visitors be brought out so that they could participate in 'homosexual intercourse' with them. Here, for the first time, the nature of the wickedness of the Sodomites that was expressed in 13:13 is fully revealed... the perversion of the whole society with blatant and widespread homosexuality was what ultimately led to the outpouring of God's wrath upon them" (Grasham 523).

The **Law of Moses** is clearer in its condemnation of homosexuality. "You shall not lie with a male as with a woman. It is an abomination" (Leviticus 18:22). "If a man lies with a male as he lies with a woman, both of them have committed an abomination. They shall surely be put to death. Their blood shall be upon them" (20:13).

The **New Testament** condemns homosexuality as a sin that will prevent one from entering Heaven. "Do you not know that the unrighteous will not inherit the kingdom of God? Do not be deceived. Neither fornicators, nor idolaters, nor adulterers, nor homosexuals, nor sodomites, nor thieves, nor covetous, nor drunkards, nor revilers, nor extortioners will inherit the kingdom of God" (1 Corinthians 6:9-10). Homosexuality is contrary to sound doctrine and the glorious gospel (1 Timothy 1:8-11) and is worthy of "suffering the vengeance of eternal fire" (Jude 7).

The Bible nowhere affirms, tolerates, sanctions, endorses or approves of homosexuality. Scripture never refers to it as an alternate lifestyle.

Homosexuality is repeatedly condemned as an abomination worthy of God's wrath.

Homosexuality violates God's law regarding gender identity, sexuality, and marriage

Men and women were created with natural sexual desires. God provided marriage as the only lawful means of fulfilling these desires (1 Corinthians 7:1-5; Hebrews 13:4). Sexual activity prior to or outside of the marriage relationship is a sin. This leads to the question, "What constitutes a marriage?"

In Matthew 19, the Pharisees asked Jesus a question about divorce. To answer the question, Jesus took them all the way back to the beginning where God established His marriage law. "And He answered and said to them, 'Have you not read that He who made them at the beginning "made them male and female," and said, "For this reason a man shall leave his father and mother and be joined to his wife, and the two shall become one flesh"? So then, they are no longer two but one flesh. Therefore what God has joined together, let not man separate'" (vv. 4-6). Some points from this passage are applicable to a study of homosexuality.

Marriage is between one man and one woman. God designed and ordained marriage, and He is the one who performs the marriage ("what God has joined together"), so He makes the rules for marriage. States and nations can change whatever laws are written on their books, but this does not change what God has written. God will not join together two men or two women. Sexual desires are to be fulfilled in marriage, and marriage is for one man and one woman.

Jesus said that God "made them male and female." A person's gender is chosen by God and is a part of his identity from the point of conception. No amount of crossdressing, hormone therapy, or sex-change operations will change the genetic markers

> **Marriage** is **honorable** among all, and the bed **undefiled**, but **fornicators** and **adulterers** God will judge.
>
> - Hebrews 13:4

that make you male or female. No person has the right to try to change his gender. Those who fear the Lord and respect His authority understand this. "But indeed, O man, who are you to reply against God? Will the thing formed say to him who formed it, 'Why have you made me like this?' Does not the potter have power over the clay..." (Romans 9:20-21).

Homosexuality is against nature

In Romans chapter one, Paul described the downward sinful spiral of the Gentiles when they departed from God. Eventually, it got to the point that, "God gave them up to vile passions. For even their women exchanged the natural use for what is against nature. Likewise also the men, leaving the natural use of the woman, burned in their lust for one another, men with men committing what is shameful, and receiving in themselves the penalty of their error which was due" (Romans 1:26-27).

Homosexuality is leaving the natural for what is against nature. A basic study of anatomy indicates that a man is suited for a woman, and a woman is suited for a man. God made them for one another. Attempting to join two women together or two men together in a sexual way is attempting what is "against nature." Plumbers and electricians know you can't put two "male" parts together or two "female" parts together. This is the "strange flesh" the men of Sodom and Gomorrah were going after (Jude 7). It was strange or unnatural for men to have sex with men. The perversion of God's natural design brought His wrath upon them.

Homosexuality brings depravity and destruction

Those who practice homosexuality receive in themselves the penalty that is due (Romans 1:27). Homosexuality is not a harmless alternate lifestyle. It is against nature. It is a perversion. One cannot go against God's natural design without suffering consequences. Homosexuals use their bodies

> ...men with men committing what is **shameful**, and receiving in themselves the **penalty** of their **error** which was due.
> - Romans 1:27

in ways God never intended. This creates physical and psychological problems.

Studies show that homosexuals are at greater risk for depression, suicide, substance abuse, HIV, and other sexually transmitted diseases. Among young people, nearly one-third (29 percent) of homosexuals have attempted suicide, compared to only 6 percent of heterosexuals (www.cdc.gov/lgbthealth/youth.htm).

Homosexuality also brings depravity upon society. Notice how all the men from every part of Sodom surrounded Lot's house to have sex with his visitors (Genesis 19:4). The men of this town were more than tolerant toward this activity; they became active participants. Like all sin, homosexuality can spread like leaven throughout a society. Repeated exposure leads to tolerance and acceptance. Some homosexuals actively target and groom prospective companions. As this sin comes to be tolerated and accepted within a society, the door opens for the acceptance of more perversions. Eventually, the moral fiber and foundation crumbles and the society is easily swept away.

Bible misrepresentations and perversions

While some homosexuals have abandoned God, the Bible, and religion altogether, others try to make the Bible allow or endorse homosexuality. Several different arguments have been made. All of them attack the truth and holiness of God and His inspired word.

- Sodom's sin was not homosexuality, but inhospitality.
- The condemnations of homosexuality in the Law of Moses apply only to practices connected with idolatry.
- David and Jonathan were homosexuals (2 Samuel 1:26).
- Ruth and Naomi were lesbians.
- The Centurion's servant that Jesus healed was a homosexual sex-slave (Matthew 8:5-13).
- Paul was a repressed homosexual.
- Jesus and the apostle John were homosexuals (John 13:23).

How tragic that people twist God's word in this manner. Indeed, "to the pure all things are pure, but to those who are defiled and unbelieving nothing is pure; but even their mind and conscience are defiled. They profess to know God, but in works they deny Him, being abominable, disobedient, and disqualified for every good work" (Titus 1:15-16).

Conclusion

The truth regarding homosexuality, same-sex marriage, gender reassignment, and any other related perversion of the patterns God set forth in His creation has been established (Psalm 119:89). These things are condemned as sins.

The Bible speaks with clarity regarding the Christian's attitude toward homosexuality and those who practice this sin. Homosexuality is a sin and we are to hate all sin (Psalm 119:128; Ephesians 5:11). Homosexuals are people made in God's image with eternal souls. They are people who need and deserve mercy, pity, and salvation. They are trapped in sin (2 Timothy 2:24-26). They need to be taught the truth and encouraged to repent.

The Bible's message for homosexuals is the same as for those who practice any sin. Forgiveness is available and can be obtained through repentance and obedience to the gospel (1 Corinthians 6:9-11).

Questions

1. How does the Bible describe the people of Sodom (Genesis 13:13; 18:20-23)? _____
   _____
   _____

2. What was the sin of the people of Sodom (Genesis 19:4-5; Jude 7)? ____
   _____

3. What did the Law of Moses say about homosexuality (Leviticus 18:22; 20:13)? _____
   _____
   _____

4. What does 1 Corinthians 6:9-10 say about those who practice homosexuality? _____
   _____
   _____

5. Where are sexual desires lawfully satisfied (1 Corinthians 7:1-5; Hebrews 13:4)? _____
   _____
   _____

LESSON 4 Homosexuality 35

6. As it pertains to our discussion of homosexuality, who will God join together in a marriage (Matthew 19:4-6)? _____
_____
_____

7. Explain why it is wrong for a person to attempt to change his gender (Matthew 19:4; Romans 9:20-21). _____
_____
_____

8. How does Paul describe homosexuality in Romans 1:26-27? _____
_____
_____

9. Have God's instructions regarding this subject ever changed (Psalm 119:89)? _____

10. What should be the Christian's attitude towards homosexuality (Psalm 119:128; Ephesians 5:11)? _____
_____
_____

11. What should be the Christian's attitude towards homosexuals (2 Timothy 2:24-26)? _____
_____
_____

12. What is the Bible's message for homosexuals (Jude 7; 1 Corinthians 6:9-11)?
_____
_____
_____

Involvement in Pornography

The word pornography is derived from the Greek word *pornographos*. This compound word (*porne* meaning "a prostitute," and *graphein* meaning "to write") literally meant "the writing of or about prostitutes." In our usage today, pornography is "sexually explicit videos, photographs, writings, or the like, whose purpose is to elicit sexual arousal" (www.dictionary.com).

Due to technological advancements, and low moral standards, pornography can be found almost everywhere in today's world. Most pornography is accessed from the internet via computers, tablets, smart phones, and other such devices.

Pornography has had a degrading effect on our society. Although numbers vary from year to year, statistics indicate that:

- There are 28,258 users watching internet pornography every second.
- Most people are exposed to pornography by the age of 18.
- On average, a young person is first exposed to pornography at the age of 11.
- Over 25% of teenagers are involved in sexting (sending, receiving, or forwarding sexually explicit messages, photographs, images or videos, primarily between mobile phones, of themselves to others).
- 90% of teens and 96% of young adults are encouraging about, accepting of, or neutral toward pornography.

> I have made a **covenant** with my **eyes**; why then should I **look upon** a young woman?
>
> - Job 31:1

> I will set **nothing wicked** before my **eyes**...
>
> - Psalm 101:3

Ours is indeed a crooked and perverse generation in which Christians must shine forth as lights in the world (Philippians 2:15). However, it may surprise us to learn that pornography isn't new. Graphic pornography existed in the first century, but it was not found in magazines or on the internet. It was displayed publicly on murals and sculptures that adorned the buildings and walkways of the cities of the Roman Empire.

"In the ruins of Pompeii are, on the walls of what were recognized as respectable homes in the first century, pictures which are painted 'engaged in such evil actions, with such devilish ingenuity of imagination, that ordinary visitors to the ruined city are not allowed to see them. When the present writer was taken, in 1913, through the new street which had just been discovered, he found that the walls of the houses fronting the street were covered with such abominable pictures that the excavator had covered them with sheets so that his working men might not be debauched by them.' In their original situation these pictures were scanned daily by the children growing up in a Graeco-Roman home! The result of such constant and degrading influence could be nothing short of debauchery. Archaeologists tell us that many of the scribblings on the walls and other surfaces in Rome and Pompeii are too obscene to appear in print. And there is no evident reason for considering these cities as exceptional; such conditions may be taken as typical of urban life in the first century" (Dana 231-232).

When the apostles condemned the "way of the Gentiles" (1 Peter 4:3; Ephesians 2:2-3; 4:17; 1 Thessalonians 4:5), pornography was very much a part of this condemned lifestyle. Today's technology has advanced, but these early Christians also struggled against pornography's influences and effects. Therefore, we can expect the New Testament to address this problem, and it does.

Pornography is a sin

We know fornication is sinful (1 Corinthians 6:9; Galatians 5:19; Ephesians 5:3-5), but where should Christians stand on pornography? Many people in our society do not think it is wrong. It is often defended as harmless fantasy, or protected as art. The word pornography isn't even found in the Bible. How can it be wrong?

As is the case with many other moral issues not specifically mentioned in the Bible, the Christian needs to understand how pornography violates principles that are set forth in Scripture.

1. **Pornography violates principles of holiness.**
   Christians are called to be holy as God is holy (1 Peter 1:15-16). We are to cleanse ourselves of the sinful filth of this world and perfect holiness in our lives (2 Corinthians 7:1). Pornography is an obstacle to perfecting and maintaining holiness. Three words (lust, uncleanness, and lewdness) often found together condemn participation in pornography.

   Several Greek words are translated as lust in the New Testament. These words all refer to a strong but morally neutral desire, craving, or longing. The context in which they are found indicates whether the desire is good or bad. Obviously, it is wrong for us to act upon any desire that will keep us from perfecting and maintaining holiness.

   The Christian is not to live his life pursuing the fulfillment of his lusts. We are called to a higher standard. "Let us walk properly, as in the day, not in revelry and drunkenness, not in lewdness and lust, not in strife and envy. But put on the Lord Jesus Christ, and make no provision for the flesh, to fulfill its lusts" (Romans 13:13-14). Pursuing these lusts leads to sin (James 1:14-15) and brings about God's wrath (Colossians 3:5-6).

> **Turn away** my eyes from looking at **worthless things**, and **revive** me in Your way.
> - Psalm 119:37

> To keep you from the **evil woman**, from the flattering tongue of a **seductress**. Do not **lust** after her beauty in your **heart**, nor let her **allure** you with her eyelids.
>
> - Proverbs 6:24-25

Temptation is not a sin, but it is a sin to lust after someone. "But I say to you that whoever looks at a woman to lust for her has already committed adultery with her in his heart" (Matthew 5:28).

> "When David accidentally saw Bathsheba taking a bath, he should have turned away and put the image out of his mind. Instead, he allowed the pornographic scene to 'fester' and create within him a desire to have sexual relations with her (2 Samuel 11:2-3). Pornography, by definition, is designed to engender lust and to arouse sensual appetites. It incites sexual appetites that are to be kept in check and guided in accordance with God's directives" (Miller 81).

The word uncleanness is translated from the Greek word *akatharsia*. This word was used in the Greek translation of the Old Testament to denote those things that were ceremonially unclean and, therefore, rendered one unacceptable before God. In the New Testament, the word uncleanness refers to unclean thoughts and desires, which lead to sinful actions. The word is associated with lewdness and fornication (2 Corinthians 12:21; Galatians 5:19; Ephesians 4:19).

The word lewdness is translated from the Greek word *aselgeia* (also translated as sensuality or lasciviousness in other versions of the New Testament). This word describes a person who does not practice self-restraint but rather gives free play to the impulses brought on by his desires. Vine's says the word "denotes excess, licentiousness, absence of restraint, indecency, wantonness" (Vine's 353). Thayer defines it as "unbridled lust, excess, licentiousness, lasciviousness, wantonness, outrageousness, shamelessness, insolence... wanton acts or manners, as filthy words, indecent bodily movements, unchaste handling of males and females" (Thayer 79-80). A lack of restraint regarding decency is most certainly displayed in both the production and consumption of pornography.

2. **Pornography violates *agape* love.** Four words in the Greek language can be translated using the English word love. One of these words is *eros*, from which we get the word erotic. This is the physical, sensual love represented in pornography. This word does not appear in the New Testament. The words *phileo* and *storge* referred to the love or affection between friends, family members, or countrymen.

The Greek word *agape* is not physical or emotional. It is best understood as benevolent good will toward others or seeking that which is in the best interest of others (Romans 13:9-10; Matthew 7:12). In the first century, this was a uniquely Christian idea, unappreciated in Greco-Roman society.

Pornography is contrary to *agape*. It does not seek the best interests of others. It is entirely selfish. Pornography is not harmless entertainment or fantasy. It turns real people into objects to be used to satisfy sexual desires. At best, objectifying of women in pornography is projected onto real women, thus establishing unfair standards and expectations upon them. At worst, pornography is linked to violence perpetrated against women.

> "It's no secret that much of porn is violent, but many people don't understand the extent to which porn's underlying messages influence behavior. Porn is full of people, particularly women, being disrespected, coerced, and physically and verbally abused, and that's shaping how society thinks and acts… Consumers might tell themselves that they aren't personally affected by porn, that they won't be fooled into believing its underlying messages, but studies suggest otherwise. There is clear evidence that porn makes many

> But I say to you that whoever **looks** at a woman to **lust** for her has **already** committed **adultery** with her in his **heart**.
>
> - Matthew 5:28

consumers more likely to support violence against women, to believe that women secretly enjoy being raped, and to actually be sexually aggressive in real life. The aggression may take many forms including verbally harassing or pressuring someone for sex, emotionally manipulating them, threatening to end the relationship unless they grant favors, deceiving them or lying to them about sex, or even physically assaulting them" (fightthenewdrug.org).

3. **Pornography perverts God's blessing of marital intimacy.** Pornography is a difficult temptation for many people because it appeals to a strong physical desire. Sexual desire is not unnatural, but it is unlawful when satisfied outside the marriage relationship.

The Bible warns us, "Do not stir up nor awaken love until it pleases" (Song of Solomon 2:7; 3:5; 8:4). There is a time and place for everything, including the joys of sex. The blessings of physical intimacy are to be explored and shared by the husbands and wives. Children and teens who view pornography receive a perverted description of sex. This can lead to frustration when unfair and unrealistic expectations are later brought into the marriage relationship.

Viewing pornography excites the pleasure center of the human brain. "Studies have shown that porn stimulates the same areas of the brain as addictive drugs, making the brain release the same chemicals. And just like drugs, porn triggers pathways in the brain that cause craving, leading users back for more and more extreme 'hits' to get high" (fightthenewdrug. org). The husband who continues to watch pornography is driving a wedge between himself and his spouse. She should be fulfilling her husband's natural desires (Proverbs 5:15-20).

> ...put on the Lord Jesus Christ, and make no **provision** for the **flesh**, to fulfill its **lusts**.
> - Romans 13:14

It is unrealistic and unfair to expect a godly woman to compete with pornography to fulfill her husband's desires.

How to overcome pornography

Pornography is a strong temptation, and our world provides unlimited access to this sin. Because of what it does to the habitual viewer's mind, pornography can become as addictive as any other pleasurable sin. It is dangerous. How can one avoid and overcome pornography addiction?

1. **Make a covenant with your eyes.** Pornography enters our hearts through our eyes, so we need to guard our eyes and be careful what we see. In today's world, it is easy to see nakedness and provocative dress and behavior. We should not go looking for it, and we need to decide beforehand what to do when we see it. Like Job, we need to make a covenant with our eyes (Job 31:1-4). David said, "I will set nothing wicked before my eyes" (Psalm 101:3). Solomon warned his sons against lusting after the seductress (Proverbs 6:25).

2. **Abstain from fleshly lusts.** "Beloved, I beg you as sojourners and pilgrims, abstain from fleshly lusts which war against the soul" (1 Peter 2:11). The word *abstain* is translated from the Greek word *apechomai* which means "to hold one's self off" (Thayer 57).

   We need to purposely and actively separate ourselves from the avenues through which we are tempted to look at pornography. Christians are not to present their bodies "as instruments of unrighteousness to sin" (Romans 6:13), but are to "put on the Lord Jesus Christ, and make no provision for the flesh, to fulfill its lusts" (Romans 13:14).

3. **Cleanse your heart.** As with any other sin, pornography's images and experiences find a way into the viewer's heart and mind. This defilement can be cleansed, but it takes work. "How can a young man cleanse his way? By taking heed according to Your word. With my whole heart I have sought You; oh, let me not wander from Your commandments! Your word I have hidden in my heart, that I might not sin against You" (Psalm 119:9-11). One must actively meditate on God's word, with a heart devoted to seeking His will, and a determination not to sin against Him. The time spent filling our hearts and lives with God's word will replace the defilement of sin.

4. **Pray for God's help.** God wants us to live lives that are free from sin (1 John 2:1). He is willing to help us accomplish this worthy goal. Jesus taught us to pray, "And do not lead us into temptation, but deliver us from the evil one…" (Matthew 6:13). If we sincerely ask God for His

help and guidance, He will help us overcome the sin in our lives (Psalm 119:37).

5. **Make your household accountable.** Joshua said, "But as for me and my house, we will serve the Lord" (Joshua 24:15). Satan is not above invading our homes to tempt us and attempt to destroy our lives with sin. Privacy and anonymity are breeding grounds for the sin of pornography. Make yourself and your children accountable regarding all electronic devices. Have a household rule that says texts, emails and viewing histories are available for anyone to see at any time (Hebrews 4:13). Set usage guidelines and use parental controls on the television, the internet, and other devices.

Conclusion

God expects Christians to shine as lights in a crooked and perverse generation (Philippians 2:15). The world lies under the sway of the wicked one (1 John 5:19), who has perverted every good thing that God has created and given to man.

In modern America, there is no evil more prominent than pornography. It poses a difficult battle, but we *must* fight and win. We *can* live holy lives in a crooked and perverse generation.

Questions

1. What happens when we pursue our fleshly lusts or desires (James 1:14-15)?
   _____
   _____
   _____

2. What did Jesus say about looking at a woman to lust for her (Matthew 5:28)? _____
   _____
   _____

3. What should David have done when he saw Bathsheba bathing (2 Samuel 11:2-4)? _____
   _____

4. Explain how pornography demonstrates an "absence of restraint" regarding decency. _____
   _____

LESSON 5 Involvement in Pornography 45

5. How do the Greek words *eros* and *agape* differ from one another?
   _____
   _____
   _____

6. Explain how pornography is contrary to *agape*. _____
   _____
   _____

7. Explain how viewing pornography can harm a marriage. _____
   _____
   _____

8. What had Job done to protect his character and his relationship with God (Job. 31:1)? _____
   _____
   _____

9. What warning did Solomon give to his sons (Proverbs 6:25)?_____
   _____
   _____

10. How can one cleanse his heart of the damage caused by pornography (Psalm 119:9-11)?_____
    _____
    _____

11. What are some things we can do to protect ourselves and our loved ones from pornography? _____
    _____
    _____
    _____

Dancing

As strangers and pilgrims in this world, Christians must abstain from lustful things that people around us accept and enjoy (1 Peter 2:11-12). Dancing is one of these things.

The dancing being considered in this lesson is the kind of dancing that is popular among many people in today's world—the kind that occurs at school dances, in dance clubs, and on popular television programs. Such dancing is not wholesome entertainment or harmless exercise. It is sinful and dangerous to those who seek to live holy lives.

Dancing in the Bible

The Bible does not say, "Thou shalt not dance." In fact, the Bible mentions dancing several times, sometimes in a favorable light.

1. **Dances of religious devotion.** These are dances that express religious enthusiasm and praise to God. Miriam led the women of Israel in a dance to celebrate their deliverance from Egypt (Exodus 15:20). King David danced before the ark as it was finally brought into Jerusalem (2 Samuel 6:14).

2. **Dances of joy and celebration.** The Bible mentions dances that express joy and the innocence of youth. Jesus used the illustration of children dancing as they played together (Matthew 11:16-17). An entire household danced in celebration of the Prodigal Son's return (Luke 15:25). This dancing was likened to the joy in Heaven when a sinner repents (vv. 7, 10).

> Beloved, I beg you as **sojourners** and **pilgrims**, **abstain** from fleshly **lusts** which **war** against the **soul**.
>
> - 1 Peter 2:11

> But when Herod's birthday was celebrated, the daughter of Herodias **danced** before them and **pleased** Herod.
>
> - Matthew 14:6

In these examples, dancing was not done for exercise, relaxation, to learn balance or coordination, or to express art or talent. Also, in these passages, men and women did not dance together. "While the mode of dancing is not known in detail, it is clear that men and women did not generally dance together, and there is no real evidence that they ever did. Social amusement was hardly a major purpose of dancing, and the modern method of dancing by couples is unknown" (*The Zondervan Pictorial Encyclopedia of the Bible*, vol. 2, page 12).

3. **Dances of sinful merrymaking.** These dances were suggestive and lewd. The Children of Israel danced before the golden calf in a shameful and unrestrained manner (Exodus 32:19-25). Such dancing would have mimicked the idol worship they had learned from the Egyptians. On Herod's birthday, his stepdaughter danced before him and his companions (Matthew 14:6-8). This dance pleased Herod. If it followed the Roman custom at that time, it was a lewd and sensual dance performed in immodest attire.

Galatians 5:19-21 lists the works of the flesh. The last work mentioned is revelries, which is translated from the Greek word *komos*. This Greek word is defined as "a nocturnal and riotous procession of half-drunken and frolicsome fellows who after supper parade through the streets with torches and music in honor of Bacchus or some other deity, and sing and play before the houses of their male and female friends; hence used generally, of feasts and drinking-parties that are protracted till late at night and indulge in revelry" (Thayer 367). Obviously, this would include sensual dancing.

The Bible does not give a blanket condemnation of all dancing. However, the dancing that is popular in today's world does not fit into the category of religious devotion or innocent celebration.

To discover what is wrong with dancing, we must get more specific than just looking at where the Bible mentions it. As it does with other worldly practices, the Bible sets forth principles for us to consider.

Dancing is lasciviousness

Another work of the flesh condemned in Galatians 5:19 is lasciviousness (also translated as lewdness, sensuality, and debauchery). Lasciviousness is translated from the Greek word *aselgeia*, which is defined as "excess, licentiousness, absence of restraint, indecency" (Vine's 353), and "wanton (acts or) manners, as filthy words, indecent bodily movements, unchaste handling of males and females" (Thayer 79-80). Today's popular dancing certainly fits these descriptions.

Sensuality (NASV, ESV) is a good rendering of this Greek word, in that it identifies *aselgeia* as anything that produces lust or sensual thought. Clearly, modern popular dancing produces lust and/or sensual thoughts, and is thus condemned as a work of the flesh. Therefore, it is sinful for Christians to engage in or endorse this kind of dancing.

Dancing produces sexual desire

Christians are sanctified (set apart) from those in the sinful world. We are not to seek to fulfill lustful passions as do those who are without God. We are expected to abstain from the sin of fornication by controlling our bodies in a holy and honorable manner (1 Thessalonians 4:3-5). This being the case, Christians should want to avoid modern popular dancing.

Many people in the world acknowledge a fact that some Christians try to deny—the dancing that is popular among worldly people stimulates sexual interest and appetites.

> For this is the **will of God**... that each of you should know how to **possess** his own **vessel** in **sanctification** and **honor**.
>
> - 1 Thessalonians 4:3-4

"Dancing is, according to George Bernard Shaw, 'The vertical expression of a horizontal desire legalized by music.'" (https://www.psychologytoday.com/us/blog/dance-psychology/201003/sex-and-dancing).

"Dr. J.P. Gibson (MD) said, '...the secret of the popularity of dancing (or is it a secret) is the exciting, sexual stimulation resulting from the close embrace of male and female, whether it be music in dancing or without music in petting and necking'" (quoted by Donnie V. Rader, *Searching the Scriptures*, Nov. 1990, page 7). Modern dancing is a precursor or gateway to intercourse. The stimulation felt on the dance floor is no different than that felt during petting in the back seat of a car.

Touching the body of the opposite sex as a couple sways together to music arouses sexual desire. Some girls may be unaware of this fact, but men and teenage boys certainly understand the connection between dancing and sexual stimulation. Heterosexual girls sometimes dance with each other, and think nothing of it, but heterosexual boys do not dance together. Men generally do not want their wives or girlfriends to dance with other men. They know what the other men are thinking and experiencing while they are dancing.

The world acknowledges the fact that sensual dancing leads to sexual arousal. Why would we allow and encourage our young people to participate? We should encourage them to take every precaution to avoid fornication (Romans 13:14).

Dancing is often associated with other sins

An activity's true nature is often seen in the company it keeps. Dancing is often accompanied by drinking and drug use. This occurs openly in clubs, but it is often present at school dances.

> Not all teens make poor decisions on prom night, but many do. A lot of teens are looking for an opportunity to party and prom night provides the perfect storm for a catastrophic event to occur. The American Automobile Association (AAA) surveyed teens aged 16-19, and 31% reported they or their friends would use drugs or alcohol during prom and graduation season. Approximately 53% of teens who admitted to drinking during or after the prom said they consumed four or more alcoholic beverages (https://www.psychologytoday.com/us/blog/teen-angst/201703/prom-and-the-afterparty).

Please note the following admission made by a high school principal in a letter sent to parents concerning the prom:

> Dear Parent(s)
>
> On April 24, 2004 the Junior-Senior Prom will be held at the Commonwealth Convention Center in Louisville, Kentucky. The prom will start at 8:00 and end at 12:00...Unfortunately, one of the things associated with the prom is the use of drugs and alcoholic beverages... The purpose of this letter is to inform you of our intent and effort to ensure the safety of your child. If a student or his/her guest chooses to come to the prom under the influence of alcohol or drugs, and this influence is detected, we will use special precautions to protect the student and those around him/her. We will detain the student and keep him/her under our supervision until parents come and get him/her.

Another sin—fornication—is commonly associated with the prom "afterparty." "In a study surveying 12,843 high school students, 14% of girls reported having sex on prom night, and 5% of those girls and 3% of boys lost their virginity on prom night" (https://www.psychologytoday.com/us/blog/teen-angst/201703/prom-and-the-afterparty).

The world openly acknowledges what some Christians deny. Dances, even school-sponsored dances, are looked upon as opportunities to engage in and enjoy different kinds of sins.

Participation in dancing causes one to be a stumbling block

One may respond, "Dancing doesn't affect me. It doesn't cause me to have lustful thoughts or desires." Any man who says this is not being honest with himself. However, if we assume it to be, a Christian knows he must also consider the influence he is having upon others.

> "Whoever causes one of these little ones who believe in Me to sin, it would be better for him if a millstone were hung around his neck, and he were drowned in the depth of the sea. Woe to the world because of offenses! For offenses must come, but woe to that man by whom the offense comes!" (Matthew 18:6-7)

Perhaps you can attend a dance and escape unharmed. If your dancing has caused others to have sexual thoughts and desires, you have become a stumbling block to them. If your participation in, and defense of, going to dances influences someone else to attend, and that person succumbs to the temptations you claim to have avoided, he has sinned; but you played a role in that sin.

Dancing harms our influence

Our participation in activities is seen as our endorsement of those activities. Therefore, Christians must be careful to maintain their influence by abstaining from the appearance of every form of evil (1 Thessalonians 5:22). We are to maintain good works so that others will see our lights (Matthew 5:16). How can you be "blameless and harmless, children of God without fault in the midst of a crooked and perverse generation, among whom you shine as lights in the world" (Philippians 2:15) if you participate in and defend dancing? How are you going to effectively talk to others about their need to repent and obey the gospel if they see you condoning something as worldly as modern popular dancing?

Conclusion

Sometimes, we may wish that the Bible spoke more plainly on moral subjects such as dancing. Wouldn't it be much easier if we could find a specific "thou shalt not" for every sinful thing we must avoid? I believe the Lord purposely avoided doing this for a good reason.

In the place of prohibitory laws, God gave us principles by which to govern ourselves. These principles require us to stop and think about our words, actions, motives, and attitudes. This causes our religion to be more than cold, heartless law-keeping. It involves our hearts and minds, which draws us closer to God.

Questions

1. Does the Bible condemn all dancing? _____

2. What are the consequences of practicing the works of the flesh (Galatians 5:19-21)? _____
   _____
   _____

3. One of the works of the flesh is lasciviousness, translated from the Greek word *aselgeia*. How is this Greek word defined? _____
   _____
   _____

4. What sins and dangers does the world associate with dances and modern dancing? _____
   _____
   _____

5. Explain how sensual dancing can lead to sexual temptation. _____
   _____
   _____

6. Is it alright to "flirt" with sexual thoughts and temptations (Romans 13:14; 1 Thessalonians 4:3-5)? Why or why not? _____
   _____
   _____
   _____

7. What did Jesus say about one who causes another to stumble (Matthew 18:6-7)? _____
   _____

8. Describe the different ways that attending a dance could be a stumbling block to others. _____
   _____
   _____

9. Explain why God does not have to specifically condemn something (say, "Thou shalt not...") in order for it to be sinful. _____
   _____
   _____

10. What kind of dancing does Scripture condemn? _____
    _____
    _____

Immodesty - Part 1

God's people tend, often to their own peril, to take on the characteristics of the world around them. One of the more noticeable ways in which this tendency exhibits itself is the choice to wear immodest clothing. This lesson considers immodest dress. Lesson 8 will address immodesty in a broader sense.

Some people in the world acknowledge the dangers of immodest dress. Consider carefully the following instructions regarding the dress code for individuals who visit inmates in Ohio prisons.

Dress code/contact rules for visitors of Ohio inmates

All prisons in Ohio follow a dress code. The dress code is for the order, safety and security of visitors, inmates and staff, and is strictly adhered to. Failure to follow the dress code will result in your visit being denied. We suggest you always bring a change of clothes with you and leave them in your car. This enables you to quickly change if a staff member objects to an article of clothing you are wearing and prevents you from potentially missing out on a visit.

- All visitors must wear appropriate undergarments, underwear, bra, slip, etc.
- Underwear should not be visible during visits.
- No clothes should expose the midriff, back, shoulders, cleavage, thighs or sides.
- Sleeveless clothing, including halter tops, tank tops, tube tops is not allowed.

> Were they **ashamed** when they had committed **abomination**? No! They were not at all ashamed; Nor did they know how to **blush**.
> - Jeremiah 6:15a

- Low-cut clothing that exposes the stomach, underwear, buttocks or chest is not allowed.
- Dresses, shorts, skirts, culottes etc., must not have a hem or slit above the middle of the knee.
- Wrap skirts, dresses, and break away pants are not allowed.
- Tight/form fitting clothing such as spandex, leggings, Lycra, including tight jeans, tight pants, leotards, unitards, or clothing that is see through, sheer or netted is not allowed.
- Excessive jewelry is not allowed, and may make the metal detector go off and require a more intrusive search.
- Clothing with gang symbols, or that is associated as gang-wear is prohibited.
- If your clothing contains offensive language or images you will not be allowed to visit.

(http://www.prisonpro.com/content/visiting-inmate-ohio)

These guidelines present the dress code in clear language, inform visitors that it will be strictly enforced, and explain why this is so: "for the order, safety and security of our visitors, inmates and staff."

The rules regarding gang symbols, offensive language, and excessive jewelry are understandable; but notice that most of the rules pertain to the exposure of the body. There is a connection between revealing clothing and the safety of the people in the facility. The state prison systems understand this. Unfortunately, some Christians are unwilling to admit the inherent danger of immodest dress.

What is so dangerous about dressing immodestly?

Immodest dress is rebellion against God

Some believe that God has not revealed an absolute standard regarding clothing or how much of the body to cover. To them, hemlines are a matter of Christian liberty, and those who insist on specifics regarding dress draw lines where God has not. However, a careful study of Scripture reveals otherwise. God gave us our bodies, and He told us how to dress and which body parts to cover.

Before sin entered the world, man was innocent; he was naked and unashamed (Genesis 2:25). When Adam and Eve sinned, their eyes were opened, they knew they were naked, and they sought to cover themselves

(Genesis 3:7). They sewed fig leaves together and made themselves "coverings," "aprons" (KJV), or "loin coverings" (NASU). "Coverings" is translated from the Hebrew word *chagowr*, which refers to a girdle, apron, or loin cloth. These make-shift clothes covered only the area around their waists. Even with these "coverings," Adam admitted he was "naked" (v. 10).

Before driving Adam and Eve from His presence, God "made tunics of skin, and clothed them" (Genesis 3:21). The Hebrew word for "tunic" (*kethoneth*) refers to a long shirt-like garment. "A tunic, the basic outer garment worn next to the skin, was a long shirt reaching the knees or ankles" (Wenham 84). It was "a tunic that was worn next to a person's body, often with long or half sleeves and reaching to the knees or ankles" (Grasham 142).

When God clothed man, He covered him from his shoulders to his knees. This is where God drew the line regarding which parts of the body He wanted covered. Purposely revealing what God covered is rebellion against God.

Immodest dress reveals nakedness

We have already learned that one does not have to be completely nude to be naked in a Scriptural sense (Genesis 3:7, 10). We can wear clothing and still be naked. What parts of the body does God expect us to cover?

1. **The thigh.** Regarding the clothing for the priests, God instructed, "And you shall make for them linen trousers to cover their nakedness; they shall reach from the waist to the thighs" (Exodus 28:42). In prophesying against Babylon, God said, "Take the millstones and grind meal. Remove your veil, take off the skirt, uncover the thigh, pass through the rivers. Your nakedness shall be uncovered, yes, your shame will be seen..." (Isaiah 47:2-3).

> Then the eyes of both of them were opened, and they knew that they were **naked**; and they sewed fig leaves together and made themselves **coverings**.
>
> - Genesis 3:7

To reveal the flesh or form of the thigh is to be naked. Clothing (short shorts, spandex or leggings, torn jeans, high slits in skirts, cheerleading uniforms, gymnastics uniforms, etc.) that does so is immodest.

2. **The buttocks.** Through the prophet Isaiah, God said the nation of Assyria would humiliate Ethiopia and Egypt. "So shall the king of Assyria lead away the Egyptians as prisoners and the Ethiopians as captives, young and old, naked and barefoot, with their buttocks uncovered, to the shame of Egypt" (Isaiah 20:4). To expose the buttocks is to be naked. Clothing that reveals the flesh or draws undue attention to the buttocks (short shorts, swimsuits, spandex or leggings, pants hanging off the waist, etc.) is immodest.

3. **The breasts.** Through the prophet Ezekiel, God spoke of how He discovered Israel as an abandoned babe, rescued her, and watched her grow. "I made you thrive like a plant in the field; and you grew, matured, and became very beautiful. Your breasts were formed, your hair grew, but you were naked and bare" (Ezekiel 16:7). To expose the breasts is to be naked. This is true for a man, as well as for a woman. Clothing that reveals the flesh or draws undue attention to the form of the breasts (low-cut blouses, tight shirts, tube tops, swimsuits, etc.) is immodest.

The Bible tells us that certain parts of the body need to be covered. To expose the thighs, buttocks, or breasts is to be naked. Notice also, that God associates shame with nakedness (Revelation 3:18; 16:15; Micah 1:11; Nahum 3:5). We should be ashamed to reveal what God wants us to conceal. Unfortunately, when it comes to wearing immodest clothing, some Christians have lost their sense of shame and have forgotten how to blush (Jeremiah 6:15).

> I counsel you to buy from Me...**white garments**, that you may be **clothed**, that the **shame** of your **nakedness** may not be revealed...
>
> - Revelation 3:18

Immodest dress sends the wrong message

Clothing is purposely designed to send a message. Some clothing helps the wearer profess godliness (1 Timothy 2:10), but some sends a different kind of message.

Solomon speaks of "the attire of a harlot" (Proverbs 7:10). This is clothing that entices men and draws their sexual attention to the harlot's body. Much of today's clothing that is passed along as modern and fashionable is purposely designed with sex appeal in mind.

Refer again to the prison dress code at the beginning of this lesson. Did you notice that several specific body parts (midriff, back, shoulders, cleavage, thighs, sides, stomach, and buttocks) had to be covered? Clothing that reveals the flesh or form of certain body parts excites lust in those who are looking.

It doesn't matter where (in a prison, school, workplace, grocery store, gym, church building, etc.) one wears this type of clothing; and it doesn't matter who (a prostitute, business woman, student, teacher, wife, or mother) wears it, the clothing does what it is designed to do—send a sexual message. It is dangerous to send a message that invites sexual interest and involvement.

Immodest dress causes a Christian to be a stumbling block

God will hold us responsible for lustful thoughts we entertain in our minds. Often, the things we see produce these thoughts. David saw Bathsheba and lusted after her (2 Samuel 11:2). God held David responsible for what he did after he looked and lusted (2 Samuel 12:7, 13). Jesus warned of looking to lust. "But I say to you that whoever looks at a woman to lust for her has already committed adultery with her in his heart" (Matthew 5:28).

> Woe to the world because of **offenses**! For offenses must come, but **woe** to that man by whom the offense comes!
>
> - Matthew 18:7

Those who look are responsible for controlling their gazes and their thoughts. However, that does not mean God will not hold accountable those who give others something to look at and lust after.

Jesus pronounced a frightening woe upon those who cause others to stumble (Matthew 18:6-7). If I dress in a way that excites lust in the hearts of others, I have become a stumbling block to them. If I encourage others to dress immodestly (compliment them regarding their appearance, buy them immodest clothes, etc.), I become a stumbling block to them.

Conclusion

The human body is a wonder of God's creation. The entrance of sin into the world destroyed man's innocence and made it necessary to cover this body. Since God designed and created the body, He has the right to determine how to adorn and present it, and He has done so in His word. Let us reject worldly standards and conform our hearts and bodies to God's standard.

Questions

1. What did Adam and Eve make for themselves after they sinned and knew they were naked (Genesis 3:7)? _____
   _____

2. What did Adam acknowledge about his condition, even though he and Eve were wearing the fig leaf coverings (v. 10)? _____
   _____

3. God clothed Adam and Eve with tunics (v. 21). Describe the parts of the body that we know would have been covered by this garment. _____
   _____
   _____

4. How is immodest dress rebellion against God? _____
   _____
   _____

5. What part of the priest's body did God want covered (Exodus 28:42)?
   _____
   _____

LESSON 7 Immodesty - Part 1   61

6. What does the Bible associate with nakedness (Isaiah 20:4; 47:3; Micah 1:11; Nahum 3:5; Revelation 3:18; 16:15). _____
   _____

7. What had the people of Jeremiah's day forgotten how to do (Jeremiah 6:15)? _____

8. What kind of a message should Christians send with their clothing (1 Timothy 2:10)? _____
   _____
   _____

9. Explain why it is *sinful* to wear clothing that invites sexual attention and interest. _____
   _____
   _____

10. Explain why it is *dangerous* to wear clothing that invites sexual attention and interest. _____
    _____
    _____

11. Do prisons have the right to tell visitors how to dress? Why or why not?
    _____
    _____
    _____

12. Does God have the right to tell us how to dress? Has He done so?_____
    _____
    _____

Lesson 8

Immodesty - Part 2

In lesson 7, we looked at the danger of immodesty. The Scriptures tell us that immodest dress is a form of rebellion against God; it reveals our nakedness (for which we should feel shame); for those attempting to profess godliness, it sends the wrong message; and it can cause others to stumble.

In this lesson we define modesty, look at principles associated with modesty, and make specific applications to our appearance and dress.

Modesty

In his first letter to Timothy, Paul wrote, "In like manner also, that the women adorn themselves in modest apparel, with propriety and moderation, not with braided hair or gold or pearls or costly clothing, but, which is proper for women professing godliness, with good works" (1 Timothy 2:9-10). In this passage, the apostle taught that the character of the men leading in the worship service ("lifting up holy hands, without wrath or doubting"—v. 8) is to be accompanied by the godly character of the women. Specifically, they are to adorn themselves in modest apparel.

1. **Modest.** The word modest is translated from the Greek word *kosmios*. This word means "orderly, well-arranged, decent" (Vine 414). While it certainly has reference to a person's clothing, the term has a much broader application. "The well ordering is not of dress and demeanor only, but of the inner life; uttering indeed and expressing itself in the outward conversation" (Trench, as quoted by Vine 414).

> In like manner also, that the women adorn themselves in **modest apparel**, with **propriety** and **moderation**, not with braided hair or gold or pearls or costly clothing, but, which is **proper** for women professing **godliness**, with **good works**.
> - 1 Timothy 2:9-10

Modest is "a state of mind or disposition that expresses a humble estimation of one's self before God. Modesty, like humility, is the opposite of boldness or arrogance. It doesn't seek to draw attention to itself or to show off in an unseemly way" (Pollard 19). When applied to our dress, we will not choose clothing that draws undue attention to ourselves.

Christians exist in various cultures, and these cultures change over time. However, human cultures do not override God's law. God has already determined what constitutes nakedness, and Christians are to abide by His divinely ordained standards. Modesty also calls for Christians to consider what is appropriate in given situations. Dressing in a way that attracts undue attention to oneself is dressing immodestly. This can be done by underdressing and by overdressing; this was the specific situation that Paul addressed in his letter to Timothy. Paul said a woman's adorning was not to be "with braided hair or gold or pearls or costly clothing" (1 Timothy 2:9). This does not mean it is a sin for a Christian woman to braid her hair, wear jewelry, or wear expensive clothing. Paul was speaking of "the elaborate hairdos of Roman society. The hair was piled high and decorated with costly jewels. No expense was spared to make them dazzling… Pliny the Elder illustrated such extravagance with the example of Lollia Paulina, who became the third wife of the emperor Caligula. Even when she attended an ordinary banquet, she was covered with emeralds and pearls interlaced alternately and shining all over her head, hair, ears, neck, and fingers" (Roper 109).

2. **Propriety.** The word propriety is translated from the Greek word *aidos*. The King James Version renders it as "shamefacedness." Although we do not often use this word, it is a good translation of this Greek word. *Aidos* is "a sense of shame" (Vine 568).

"Walter Bauer's lexicon says, 'This term expresses… a respect for convention' and then lists an example: 'modesty of women.' Let us consider the phrase 'a respect for convention.' 'Convention' is 'general usage or custom,' 'an accepted or prescribed practice.' It is a general agreement in whatever society we find ourselves. In this case, the word is referring to a general agreement regarding women's clothing. Paul is not suggesting that a Christian woman should be guided by what society decrees is respectable clothing (see Romans 12:2), but he was indicating that a Christian woman should never wear anything frowned on by society. In that sense, she should have 'a respect for convention'" (Roper 108).

The word propriety indicates that lines have been drawn to define what is acceptable, and what is unacceptable. Christians are to recognize where these lines are drawn and feel shame when they cross them.

3. **Moderation.** The word moderation is translated from the Greek word *sophrosune*. This word refers to "soundness of mind, self-control" (Thayer 613). It "signifies a command over bodily passions, a state of self-mastery in the area of the appetite. The basic meaning of the word has different nuances and connotations and represents that habitual inner self-government, with its constant rein on all the passions and desires, which would hinder the temptation to immodesty from arising" (Pollard 20).

These three words (modesty, propriety, and moderation) work together to guide a Christian in choosing his or her wardrobe. Modesty is the desire to have everything orderly and well arranged; propriety tells us to recognize acceptable standards; and moderation calls for us to abide within these standards.

When culture and creed collide

Since cultures sometimes indicate that revealing clothing is acceptable in given situations, Christians need to be aware of the God-drawn lines regarding nakedness. For instance, in many cultures it is normal for people to wear revealing clothing at a swimming pool or beach. When a Christian wears such swimwear, he may be fitting in with the crowd; but he is also violating the principles regarding nakedness discussed in the previous chapter. The young Christian woman in her backless, strapless formal may be dressed just like all the other young women, but she is exposing parts of her body that God intended for her to have covered. Being near a body of water, in a wedding, or at a formal event does not negate God's teaching regarding nakedness.

> And do not be **conformed** to this **world**, but be **transformed** by the renewing of your mind, that you may prove what is that **good** and **acceptable** and **perfect will** of God.
>
> - Romans 12:2

Where I once lived, the school system implemented a dress code. An article in the newspaper stated that students had to cover specific body parts, including thighs and midriffs. I called the school and asked if this change in the dress code would ban outfits worn by cheerleaders and student athletes. I was told that, although these outfits did reveal these body parts, they were not banned because they were considered "uniforms." Calling something a "uniform" does not mean the person wearing it is no longer naked. Revealing clothing sends the same message, regardless whether it is culturally acceptable to wear the clothing in given situations.

Tattoos and body piercings

In our culture, tattoos have become a very popular trend. "People get tattoos for many reasons: for attention, self-expression, artistic freedom, rebellion, a visual display of a personal narrative, reminders of spiritual/cultural traditions, sexual motivation, addiction, identification with a group or even drunken impulsiveness (which is why many tattoo parlors are open late)" (https://www.huffpost.com/entry/psychology-of-tattoos_b_2017530).

What does the Bible say about Christians getting tattoos?

The only verse in the Bible that mentions tattoos is Leviticus 19:28. "You shall not make any cuttings in your flesh for the dead, nor tattoo any marks on you: I am the Lord." This verse is referring to the cultic mourning practices of pagan cultures. The Israelites were a holy people to the Lord and were not to take on the practices of the pagans around them (Deuteronomy 14:1-2). "They were not denied the right to mourn in times of loss and grief, but any rituals that might involve the disfiguring of their God-given bodies were considered trespasses against God" (Demarest 225-226).

This passage is part of the Law of Moses, which was fulfilled and taken away at the cross (Colossians 2:14). For some, this means the prohibition against tattoos has been removed. However, there are principles that Christians must consider in determining God's will regarding the modern practice of getting tattoos, body piercings, and other body alterations.

Christians must be aware of the messages their bodies are sending to others. In this world, we are to shine as lights (Philippians 2:15) and profess godliness (1 Timothy 2:10). Just as provocative attire sends a message that you are inviting sexual interest, tattoos also send a message.

"In studying first impressions of people that have tattoos, researchers have found that avatars (neutral) with tattoos and other body modifications were rated as more likely to be thrill and adventure seekers, to have a higher number of previous sexual partners, and to be less inhibited than

LESSON 8 Immodesty - Part 2

non-tattooed avatars. This study looked at general stigma associated with people sporting tattoos" (https://www.huffpost.com/entry/psychology-of-tattoos_b_2017530).

Those getting tattoos for their shock value are demonstrating one definition of immodesty. They are purposely (and permanently) drawing undue attention to themselves. Christians should not want to send these kinds of messages to the world around them.

Tattoos are growing in popularity and are becoming more acceptable in our society. The stigma that once accompanied them is slowly disappearing. There may come a day when tattoos and body piercings become normal, at which time a Christian wearing them will not be considered immodest. However, no Christian should find himself on the cutting edge of societal or cultural changes. Those who do so draw attention to themselves, which is a violation of God's modesty law.

Some people see their bodies as their own canvases or journals upon which to record their thoughts and messages for the world to read. This is not a scriptural view of the Christian's body. Our physical bodies are not our own. They belong to God (1 Corinthians 6:19-20).

If a friend loans me his car, I may have possession of it for a while, but I do not own it. The car does not belong to me. I don't have the right to cover it with bumper stickers that reflect my views, opinions, hobbies, family members' names, favorite music groups or sports teams. Neither do I have the right to take God's body and cover it with artwork of my own choosing.

Tattoos and other body alterations (such as wearing gages in the ears) are permanent. Tattoos may be growing in popularity, but so is tattoo removal. Statistics indicate that as many as 25% of people who get tattoos regret their decisions. These tattoos can be removed, but the process is both expensive and painful.

> Or do you not know that your **body** is the temple of the **Holy Spirit** who is in you, whom you have from God, and you **are not your own**?
>
> - 1 Corinthians 6:19

What about people who decide to get tattoos before they become Christians? Obviously, baptism does not wash away these physical marks. They are part of the life lived without Christ, a life now redeemed and being used for God's glory. They are not different from other past decisions with which one must live after becoming a follower of Christ.

Conclusion

The way we appear before others must be consistent with our claim to be disciples of Christ. In the absence of a dress code, the Bible gives principles to govern the Christian's appearance. While it is not wrong to follow the fashions of the cultures in which we live, Christians must never be on the cutting edge of changes in societal norms. Likewise, the faithful Christian will always dress in such a way as to cover his or her nakedness and be pleasing in God's sight.

Questions

1. What does the word modest (*kosmios*) mean? _____
   _____
   _____

2. Could a person have his or her body adequately covered and still be immodest (1 Timothy 2:9)? Why or why not? _____
   _____
   _____
   _____

3. What kind of statement should a Christian want to make with his or her clothing and appearance (1 Timothy 2:10)? _____
   _____
   _____
   _____

4. What does the word propriety or shamefacedness (*aidos*) mean? _____
   _____
   _____

5. What does the word moderation (*sophrosune*) mean? _____
   _____
   _____

LESSON 8 Immodesty - Part 2

6. Explain how the principles of modesty, propriety, and moderation work together to shape a Christian's appearance to the world. _____

   _____
   _____
   _____
   _____

7. Is it all right for a Christian to wear a bikini, short shorts, cheerleader uniform, backless gown, etc., if everyone else is wearing one? Why or why not? _____

   _____
   _____
   _____

8. What are some reasons people give for getting tattoos? _____

   _____
   _____
   _____
   _____

9. What messages have tattoos been proven to send? _____

   _____
   _____
   _____

10. Explain why the Christian's body is not a personal canvas or journal upon which to record thoughts and messages for the world to read (1 Corinthians 6:19-20). _____

    _____
    _____
    _____

11. What advice would you give a young Christian who is considering getting a tattoo? _____

    _____
    _____
    _____

Gambling

Gambling is a prominent part of today's culture. Estimates indicate that 60 percent of the people in the United States gamble regularly. Eighty percent of Americans approve of legalized gambling. Every year they spend billions of dollars on gambling.

In a growing number of states, the citizens can now enjoy, in legalized casinos and at race tracks, gambling activities that were once reserved for late night in back rooms. The number of gambling websites is constantly increasing. One can buy a lottery ticket at the corner convenience story, take part in an office pool, or even engage in church-sponsored gambling activities.

Since gambling is so popular, and participation is so easy, it behooves us to consider what the Bible says about this activity. Is it a harmless form of entertainment, or is it a dangerous sin?

What is gambling?

Sometimes, people seek to justify gambling with such arguments as, "We gamble every time we cross the street, invest in the stock market, or buy a used car." The gambling we are considering in this lesson does not apply to every activity that involves taking a chance or a risk.

> "A person engages in gambling if he stakes or risks something of value upon the outcome of a contest of chance or a future contingent event not under his control or influence, upon an agreement or understanding that he or someone else will receive something of value in the event of a certain outcome. Gambling does not include bona fide business transactions valid under the

> Let him who stole **steal no longer**, but rather let him **labor**, working with his hands what is **good**, that he may have something to **give** him who has **need**.
>
> - Ephesians 4:28

law of contracts, such as the purchase or sale at a future date of securities or commodities, contracts of indemnity or guaranty and life, health or accident insurance" (https://definitions.uslegal.com/g/gambling).

Although the word "gambling" does not appear in the Bible, Christians must understand that gambling is condemned as a sin. The Bible sets forth principles that must govern a Christian's thoughts and actions. Several things an honest person can observe about gambling show it to be a sinful activity.

Gambling violates principles of righteousness

> If anyone will not **work**, neither shall he **eat**.
> - 2 Thessalonians 3:10b

1. **Gambling violates the authorized means of gaining wealth.** It is not a sin to gain money or to possess wealth, but such must be obtained in a scriptural manner. We can *earn wages* from honest work (Luke 10:7, Ephesians 4:28, 2 Thessalonians 3:10). We can make money when we *sell* something (Matthew 13:44, Acts 4:34-37, James 4:13). We can receive a *gift* (Ephesians 4:28, Matthew 2:11, Acts 20:35) or an *inheritance* (Numbers 27:1-11, Deuteronomy 21:15-17, Luke 15:12).

   God does not authorize man to gain wealth by wagering on events or investing in get-rich-quick schemes.

2. **Gambling violates the principle of stewardship.** Everything we have comes from God, and still belongs to God (Psalms 24:1). Christians are stewards of God's blessings (1 Peter 4:10), and stewards must be faithful in their oversight of those things that are under their charge (1 Corinthians 4:1-2). There is a sense in which the things we have belong to us (Acts 5:4), but we must use them in the way that God allows. He does not allow us to squander our possessions through gambling. The odds are

always in the house's favor. We are literally "throwing money away" when we gamble—money that actually belongs to God.

3. **Gambling violates the principle of brotherly love.** The only way for one person to win at gambling is for another to lose his wager. The experienced gambler uses his skills to exploit the less experienced and take their money. He does not care about those who lose. Thus, gambling is a combination of stealing and selfishness. Gambling has been called "stealing by consent" because the losers are willing participants, but it is still stealing.

We are to love our neighbor as ourselves (Matthew 22:39). We are to do to them as we want them to do to us (Matthew 7:12). Love does no harm to one's fellow man (Romans 13:10), but gambling takes that which belongs to another. These principles destroy the basis upon which gambling is established.

The motivation behind gambling is sinful

Some people justify their involvement in gambling by considering it to be innocent entertainment. They may walk away from the casino with empty pockets, but they view their lost money as having been "spent" on entertainment. We have already shown that gambling is not innocent fun. It is an effort to take that which belongs to someone else. However, some elements involved in gambling make it exciting and entertaining to some people, and it is these enticements which also make it sinful.

1. **Greed.** The true appeal behind gambling is the possibility of hitting it big and getting rich. Casinos lure gamblers with promises of the "Biggest Payoffs" and the "Loosest Slots in Town." It is no accident that more lottery tickets are sold as the jackpots get bigger.

   The Bible warns against the desire to be rich. "But those who desire to be rich fall into temptation and a snare, and into many foolish and harmful lusts which drown men in destruction and perdition. For the love of money is a root of all kinds of evil, for which some have strayed from the faith in their greediness, and pierced themselves through with many sorrows" (1 Timothy 6:9-10). A love of money and a desire to become rich can entice a Christian to become involved in, and carried away by, the sin of gambling. Greed creates a monster that is never satisfied (Ecclesiastes 5:10-12).

2. **Covetousness.** To covet is to be eager to have more, especially that which belongs to someone else. Jesus taught us to beware of covetousness (Luke 12:15). The Bible calls covetousness "idolatry,"

> For this you know, that no...**covetous** man, who is an **idolater**, has any inheritance in the **kingdom** of Christ and God.
>
> - Ephesians 5:5

condemns it as a sin worthy of God's wrath, and tells us to avoid it (Ephesians 5:3-7, Colossians 3:5-6).

Some people may gamble because they enjoy the competition, or see it as a form of entertainment; but one wonders how many would participate in this "entertainment" if they knew they wouldn't be allowed to keep their winnings?

The fruit of gambling is sinful

Sometimes the sinfulness of an activity can be seen in the fruit that it produces. Consider the following fruits of gambling.

1. **Gambling is addictive.** The very fact that there is an organization called "Gamblers Anonymous" proves this point. Some people are unable to walk away from a casino. Gambling can maintain a grip on some people in much the same way as drugs and alcohol. Statistics indicate that millions of people display signs of gambling addiction. Even those who supply the gambling opportunities acknowledge this and provide telephone numbers for those who need help with their addiction.

   The Christian is not to allow anything, including the desire to gamble, to have control over himself. "All things are lawful for me, but all things are not helpful. All things are lawful for me, but I will not be brought under the power of any" (1 Corinthians 6:12).

2. **Gambling destroys lives.** Problem gamblers lose more than their wages. While specific numbers may vary from year to year, statistics indicate that problem gamblers incur debt, commit crimes to support their addiction, have a divorce rate nearly double that of nongamblers, and are 20 times more likely to commit suicide than nongamblers.

3. **Gamblers have evil companions.** "He who walks with wise men will be wise, but the companion of fools will be destroyed" (Proverbs 13:20). Instead of surrounding themselves with brethren who are striving to go to Heaven, Christians who gamble are associating with, and being influenced by, people who are motivated by greed and covetousness (1 Corinthians 15:33). These people are not trying to help others get to Heaven. They are seeking to exploit them and take their money.

4. **Gambling contributes to crime and other sins.** We have heard the catch-phrase: "What happens in Vegas stays in Vegas!" What is happening in Vegas that people don't want the folks back home to know about?

   Which came to Vegas first—the crime, drugs, and prostitution, or the casinos? After casinos opened in Atlantic City, the total number of crimes within a 30 mile radius increased 100 percent.

5. **Gambling destroys a person's influence.** The Christian must be careful to maintain an influence for good in this world (Matthew 5:13-16). While the world at large may view gambling as harmless entertainment, those who have eaten its bitter fruits know the pain it can bring. The Christian who engages in this sin, or condones it in the lives of others, can become a stumbling block. We must "become blameless and harmless, children of God without fault in the midst of a crooked and perverse generation, among whom you shine as lights in the world" (Philippians 2:15).

   Jesus said a tree is known by its fruits (Matthew 12:33), and gambling's fruit is evil. Christians must not be associated with this sin.

Conclusion

Some try to justify their involvement in gambling by arguing that we take chances in several different areas in our lives: driving, crossing the street, farming, investing, buying insurance, etc.

Remember, gambling involves more than taking a chance. Gambling involves risking a wager as a means of taking something of value from someone else. The farmer does not profit at another's misfortune. The investor profits when the company profits (everyone wins). Satan is the only one who truly profits from gambling. Everyone else eventually loses.

Questions

1. What is gambling? _____
   _____
   _____

Overcoming Worldliness

2. What are the legitimate, God-authorized ways for us to increase our wealth? Provide scriptures to support your answers. _____
_____
_____

3. To whom does our money really belong (1 Peter 4:10)? _____
_____

4. What characteristic is required of stewards (1 Corinthians 4:1-2)? _____
_____
_____

5. Explain why gambling is a violation of the command to love our neighbors (Matthew 22:39; Romans 13:8-10). _____
_____
_____

6. What is the true motivation behind gambling? _____
_____
_____

7. List some things the Bible has to say about the sin of covetousness (Luke 12:15; Ephesians 5:3-7; Colossians 3:5-6). _____
_____
_____
_____

8. Discuss some of the "fruits" of gambling. _____
_____
_____
_____

9. The Bible never uses the word "gambling." Explain how we can know gambling is a sin when it is not specifically mentioned in the Bible.
_____
_____
_____

Materialism

Materialism is one of many worldly dangers that threaten Christians. This sin's seriousness is in its subtlety. Unlike blatantly obvious sins such as drug use, fornication, and homosexuality, materialism is an unseen enemy. Most people are aware that it exists, but they are ignorant of its true potential and danger.

Materialism is defined as a "preoccupation with or emphasis on material objects, comforts, and considerations, with a disinterest in or rejection of spiritual, intellectual, or cultural values" (www.dictionary.com). It is the idea that life's highest value is to be achieved in material pursuits and progress.

Materialism is "an outlook on life leaving God out or making Him secondary to this material world. It casts man's spiritual nature into second place and his physical desires into first. This is a recipe for sin of every sort" (Blackaby 53).

We see the influence of materialism all around us—in our advertising and entertainment, in the things we value, and the way we look upon ourselves and others. It has even found its way into modern religion. The "Health and Wealth" gospel (the belief that God will reward one's faith with an abundance of material wealth in this life) is the result of materialism.

> He who **loves silver** will not be **satisfied** with silver; nor he who **loves abundance**, with **increase**. This also is **vanity**.
>
> - Ecclesiastes 5:10

Why materialism is dangerous

We live in a physical world. Our bodies require physical things for survival. What is wrong with materialism? What makes it something to overcome and avoid?

> Take heed and **beware** of **covetousness**, for one's life does not consist in the **abundance** of the things he **possesses**.
> - Luke 12:15

1. **Materialism cannot deliver what it promises.** Advertisers spend billions of dollars to convince us we need things in order to be happy and fulfilled. Many people believe success, peace of mind, and self-worth will come if they have wealth or a comfortable abundance of things. Materialism promises, but it cannot deliver.

   King Solomon had the unique opportunity to pursue materialism to its fullest extent (Ecclesiastes 2:1-11). He filled his life with pleasure, fine dining, beautiful homes, numerous servants, great herds and flocks, riches, entertainment, and power. He had it all, but he learned a sobering lesson. "Then I looked on all the works that my hands had done and on the labor in which I had toiled; and indeed all was vanity and grasping for the wind. There was no profit under the sun" (Ecclesiastes 2:11).

   Solomon discovered that acquiring wealth does not solve life's problems—it creates them. Obtaining material things will never satisfy a covetous longing for those things. Amassed wealth and property requires management and upkeep, which robs a man of his peace (Ecclesiastes 5:10-12). Material wealth does not provide more time to spend with family and in doing the Lord's work. It drains our time and energy. It does not make life easier; nor does it bring lasting happiness.

2. **Materialism blinds us to our spiritual needs and responsibilities.** On one occasion, a man asked Jesus to make his brother divide an inheritance with him (Luke 12:13-21). Jesus refused to get involved in this matter, then sounded forth a warning against this man's attitude: "Take heed and beware of covetousness, for one's life does not consist in the abundance of the things he possesses" (v. 15). The parable that followed illustrates this danger.

Covetousness had made this man selfish. He made no reference to God or to others who might be in need. He did not seek to make proper use of his surplus (1 Timothy 6:17-19). He thought only of himself. This man also mistook his body for his soul (v. 19). He was fixated on the here and now, and gave no thought to his eternal soul or his accountability to God.

Man is a spiritual being who lives for a brief time, in a physical body, in a physical world. Solomon learned that life is not about accumulating things, but about preparing to meet your God (Ecclesiastes 12:13-14). Materialism blinds man to this reality and renders him woefully unprepared for eternity.

3. **Materialism affects the way we treat others.** This world attaches undue importance upon material wealth and status. Materialists "judge others based on their power, their ability to help us materially or the honors their association brings, rather than assessing people on the basis of spiritual factors, like their love, goodness, kindness, self-control, and faithfulness" (Blackaby 64). Any of us can easily fall into this trap.

James presents a scenario in which two unknown visitors enter the assembly of the church (James 2:2-9). One appears to be wealthy and the other poor. The rich man is honored, while the poor man is "dishonored" (v. 6).

Materialism turns people into objects. James said they had shown partiality because they had "become judges with evil thoughts" (v. 4). They were kind to the rich man because they believed he could be a benefit to them. They dismissed the poor man because they did not find him useful.

The Gospel calls upon us to love all men because they are created in God's image and possess eternal souls. We are to treat others with love, honor, and respect—the way we want to be treated (Matthew 7:12).

4. **Materialism prevents spiritual growth and fruitfulness.** God expects Christians to grow and produce fruit to His glory (1 Peter 2:1-2; Hebrews 5:12-14; John 15:1-8). Materialism is the enemy of such growth.

In the Parable of the Sower, the thorny ground represents the crowded or preoccupied heart. The seed takes root and begins to grow, but it cannot grow to maturity or produce fruit because it cannot compete with the other plants aggressively taking the soil's space and nutrients.

Luke's account tells us there are three things that choke the word out of the believer's heart (Luke 8:14). *Cares* are the selfish or excessive worries over our own welfare (Matthew 6:25-34). *Riches* are material

> For the **love of money** is a root of all kinds of **evil**, for which some have **strayed** from the faith in their **greediness**, and pierced themselves through with many **sorrows**.
>
> - 1 Timothy 6:10

things. Both the desire to obtain them and the effort to maintain them choke out the word. *Pleasures of life* is "a phrase referring to the fleeting enjoyment of that which is tied to one's earthly existence as opposed to eternal spiritual blessing" (Caldwell 482). These can be sinful pleasures or an overindulgence in innocent pleasures such as entertainment or recreation. Preoccupation with these things makes it impossible to produce fruit.

5. **Materialism draws us away from the faith.** It is not a sin to possess wealth, but it is dangerous to "desire to be rich" and to possess a "love of money" (1 Timothy 6:9-10). Please note, one does not have to be rich to desire riches, neither does he have to possess money to love money. The danger is greed and covetousness.

Paul spares no detail in describing the fate of the covetous man. He falls into temptation and a snare. Like a wild animal following his appetite, he has landed in a trap from which he cannot escape. His greed pulled him under, and he drowned or plunged into ruin and destruction. He wandered or strayed from the faith. He didn't leave overnight. Materialism slowly pulled him away from following the Lord. Finally, he is impaled on the fruits of his greediness. The word pierced is translated from the Greek word *peripeiro* which means to penetrate entirely. "To put on a spit, hence, 'to pierce,' is used metaphorically in 1 Timothy 6:10, of torturing one's soul with many sorrows" (Vine's 471). Like a pig roasting over a pit, so is the end of the covetous man. He is impaled and finds sorrow, grief, and pain at every turn.

Overcoming materialism

This may be more difficult than we think. We live in a materialistic world and need material things for our physical bodies to survive. Even the church needs money to do its work. Where do we draw the line between an overemphasis on material objects and making proper use of material blessings available to us?

The Bible has a lot to say about riches, material possessions, and where the Christian should place his emphasis. In fact, Jesus addressed materialism in a large portion of His Sermon on the Mount (Matthew 6:19-34). These verses provide a good starting place for addressing and overcoming materialism.

1. **Establish the right priorities (Matthew 6:19-21).** Jesus is not forbidding man from working, owning material possessions, or even saving up for the future. The *treasure* in this passage is that which we value above all other things, the supreme focus of our hearts (v. 21). It is important that we focus our hearts on the right things (Proverbs 4:23). Materialism moves the Christian's focus away from spiritual priorities, thus robbing him of his spiritual blessings.

   Earthly treasures do not last. Physical things are subject to theft and decay. Material possessions can be taken from us (Proverbs 23:4-5). Most of them end up in the garbage dump. They bring no lasting satisfaction (Ecclesiastes 5:10-12).

   Laying up treasure in heaven is not making payments toward a meritorious eternal reward. It is submitting oneself completely to that which is in heaven—God's rule and authority. It is the life-long pursuit of spiritual things (Colossians 3:1-2), the development of character (Galatians 5:22-23; 2 Peter 1:5-7), and endeavoring to help others enter Heaven. These treasures can never be taken away.

2. **Have the proper outlook (Matthew 6:22-23).** Jesus compares the eye's function for the body with the influence of one's perspective upon his heart and life. Materialism completely changes the way a man views life. If one's outlook is materialistic, his life is full of darkness.

> For where your **treasure** is, there your **heart** will be also.
>
> - Matthew 6:21

The remedy for covetousness and materialism is *contentment* (1 Timothy 6:6-8). Contentment is satisfaction with what one has. The material things of this world are not for accumulation (v. 7). They are blessings to be used as we journey through this life in preparation for eternity. Our physical bodies need material sustenance. As long as we have what we need, we are to be satisfied (v. 8).

This does not mean it is sinful for us to better ourselves, but the secret to happiness is learning to be content with what we have (Philippians 4:11), not in giving ourselves everything we want.

3. **Confirm your loyalty to God (Matthew 6:24).** *Mammon* was the common Aramaic word for wealth. Man cannot serve God and materialism. Total loyalty cannot be divided between two masters; God will not accept second place in our hearts.

   A Christian's attitude toward material things should be that of a *steward*. A steward is a manager of another person's property (Luke 16:12). All material things actually belong to God (Psalms 24:1). If they come into our possession, we must use them the way the Owner wants them to be used.

4. **Develop your trust in God (Matthew 6:25-34).** This section on worrying is a part of the Lord's teaching against materialism. While not all worries and troubles are connected to material things, many are.

   Jesus poses some arguments to illustrate how worrying about life's necessities is inconsistent with what we know about God. First, God gave us our lives. Can't we trust Him to give us the things that will sustain us (v. 25)? If God cares for little birds of the air, and grass in the fields, can't we trust Him to care for those who are of much greater value to Him (vv. 26, 28-30)? Worrying is for unbelievers (vv. 31-32). They do not know a benevolent God provides for them, but we do. Finally, worry is a thief, robbing us of today (v. 34) and of our quality of life (v. 27).

   We show our trust in God when we willingly "seek first the kingdom of God and His righteousness" (v. 33). We overcome materialism, and worry, by focusing on spiritual things. To seek first the kingdom of God is to make God's will your top priority; to truly and fully submit to Him in every aspect of your life. This will include your attitude towards, and use of, material things.

Conclusion

Materialistic attitudes and behavior are incompatible with being a citizen in the Kingdom of God. We pass through this world as strangers and pilgrims. Nothing here is ours to keep. Trying to do so will cost us our eternal souls.

Questions

1. What is materialism? _____
   _____
   _____

2. Does a person have to be wealthy to have a problem with materialism?
   _____

3. What is covetousness? Why can't materialism satisfy a covetous heart (Ecclesiastes 5:10)? _____
   _____
   _____

4. What warning does Jesus give in Luke 12:15? _____
   _____
   _____

5. Identify at least two mistakes made by the rich fool in Luke 12:16-21.
   _____
   _____

6. James says some Christians treated a rich visitor with partiality because they had evil thoughts or motives (James 2:4). What do you think these motives could have been? _____
   _____
   _____

7. What three things keep the preoccupied heart from producing fruit (Luke 8:14)? _____
   _____
   _____

8. How does Paul describe the fate of the materialistic person (1 Timothy 6:9-10)? _____
   _____
   _____

9. According to Jesus, what is one's most valuable possession (Matthew 16:26)? _____
   _____

84 Overcoming Worldliness

10. How do we lay up treasure in Heaven (Matthew 6:19-21)? _____
_____
_____
_____

11. What is contentment? Explain how learning to be content can help us overcome materialism. _____
_____
_____
_____
_____
_____

12. What is a steward? Explain how the concept of stewardship can help us overcome materialism. _____
_____
_____
_____
_____
_____

13. How can learning to trust God to care for us help us overcome materialism? _____
_____
_____
_____
_____
_____

Lesson 11

Sinful Speech

Although they may acknowledge the power of one's words, those in the world think very little about how one speaks. There was a time when filthy language and dirty stories were reserved for private conversations. If such language was spoken in public, it was soon followed by an apology. That time is long gone. Today, we hear filthy language from all kinds of people, in all kinds of places. Even Christians can be heard using such talk.

The Bible tells us to take our words seriously. Solomon said, "Death and life are in the power of the tongue, and those who love it will eat its fruit" (Proverbs 18:21). Jesus warned, "But I say to you that for every idle word men may speak, they will give account of it in the day of judgment. For by your words you will be justified, and by your words you will be condemned" (Matthew 12:36-37).

We will give an account for every idle word we speak, write, text, or send for others to see and hear. Our words have the power to justify or condemn us because the tongue is an instrument of the heart. "For out of the abundance of the heart the mouth speaks" (Matthew 12:34). The tongue is all too willing to reveal the true nature of man's heart.

There are many ways we can sin with our speech, but this lesson focuses upon the use of corrupt words, filthy talk, profanity, and euphemisms.

Corrupt words

The doctrine of Christ forbids the use of dirty words, or cussing. "Let no corrupt word proceed out of your mouth, but what is good for necessary

> The speech of a Christian should be **sound** (Titus 2:8), with great **boldness** (2 Corinthians 3:12), **gracious** and seasoned with salt (Colossians 4:6). We are to speak as the **oracles of God** (1 Peter 4:11), and we are to speak the **truth** in **love** (Ephesians 4:15).

edification, that it may impart grace to the hearers" (Ephesians 4:29).

The word *corrupt* is translated from the Greek word *sapros* which refers to that which is rotten, worthless, or unfit for use. While this would include any kind of speech (such as gossip, lying, disrespectful talk, false doctrine, etc.) that has a rotting or degrading effect upon the hearers, it certainly includes the swear words or four-letter words that we so often hear in today' society.

These words themselves are rotten, but they also have a corrupting influence on those who hear them. Every Christian must remove such words from his vocabulary.

Filthy talk

"But fornication and all uncleanness or covetousness, let it not even be named among you, as is fitting for saints; neither filthiness, nor foolish talking, nor coarse jesting, which are not fitting, but rather giving of thanks" (Ephesians 5:3-4).

Christians are not to be associated with sins such as fornication, lewdness, and covetousness. It is not fitting for those who have been set apart for God to engage in such things. However, notice how the prohibition also addresses our speech. There is to be no filthy speech, foolish talking, or crude joking. This is the type of talking engaged in by those who do not think or care about the impact their words have on others. This includes telling dirty jokes, using sexual innuendos, or retelling sinful exploits seen on TV or heard from others. This kind of talk is commonly heard in today's world, but it is not fitting for such speech to come from the mouth of a Christian. In fact, it is shameful (Ephesians 5:12).

Profanity

The word profane means "showing disrespect or contempt for sacred things, to put to a base or improper use" (*Webster's New World Dictionary*,

> For it is **shameful** even to **speak** of those things which are done by them in **secret**.
>
> - Ephesians 5:12

page 1134). Although the word profanity is often used to refer to all dirty language, it really applies to the vain use of God's name.

God left very clear instructions regarding how His name is to be used. "You shall not take the name of the Lord your God in vain, for the Lord will not hold him guiltless who takes His name in vain" (Exodus 20:7). To use God's name in vain is to use it in a common, empty, or careless manner without an attitude of sincere reverence or respect. The Law of Moses called for the death penalty as a punishment for this sin (Leviticus 24:16). Today we live under a different covenant, but we serve the same God Who demands our reverence and respect (Hebrews 12:28-29).

Not only is God's name used as a curse word today, but people use the names of God and His Son as common exclamations to express any and every emotion imaginable. Calling upon God in expressions of praise or prayer is appropriate. Using God's name when reading the Bible or teaching His word is certainly allowable. However, using God's name, or the things associated with God, as a means of mindlessly expressing surprise, pleasure, disgust, or anger is using His name in a common way. This is a sin, and God will not hold him guiltless who takes His name is vain.

Advances in technology have given today's Christians another avenue of communication—texting. To save time, texters use abbreviations in the place of entire sentences. For instance: TTYL means "talk to you later;" LOL means "laugh out loud;" BTW means "by the way." Another popular abbreviation is OMG, which stands for "Oh my God!" Every time one types in these three letters and hits "send" he is using God's name in vain. Other abbreviations include letters that stand in the place of curse words, and Christians have been observed using them in their texts and on social networking sites.

Euphemisms

A euphemism is an inoffensive expression used as a substitution for one considered to be offensive. Some have called it "Christian cussing."

To many people, words such as darn, dang, heck, shoot, shucks, gosh, golly, doggone, sheesh, gee whiz, cripes, crikey, etc., may seem to be innocent, but a dictionary will tell us what we are really saying when we use such substitute words.

While euphemisms may make for more acceptable conversation, they are not fitting for the child of God. They mean the same thing as the more offensive words, so we might as well be saying the offensive words. The use of such words betrays what is really in our hearts. The same emotions prompt their use, even if they are being filtered and toned down before they leave our mouth. Replacing offensive words with less offensive words is not appropriate for one who is striving to please God. We should be willing to remove such outbursts altogether.

Overcoming the use of corrupt speech and filthy language

Using bad language, profanity, and euphemisms is a habit, and this habit can be broken. Many Christians have done so. Following are some things you can do to help you overcome this habit:

1. **Learn to think before you speak.** "The heart of the righteous studies how to answer, but the mouth of the wicked pours forth evil" (Proverbs 15:28). A thoughtless person's mind gathers up commonly used words and sends them out of his mouth. A righteous person takes the time to think before he speaks. His thoughts are edited, and his words are carefully chosen, before they leave his mouth. We are to be swift to hear and slow to speak (James 1:19).

> ...let every man be **swift** to **hear**, **slow** to **speak**...
>
> - James 1:19

2. **Remember the power of your words.** We will give an answer for every idle word we speak (Matthew 12:26-27). Your words have the power to determine the fate of your eternal soul (Proverbs 18:21). This is a sobering fact, which should always govern the way everyone speaks.

3. **Seek to edify others with your speech.** "Let no corrupt word proceed out of your mouth, but what is good for necessary edification, that it may impart grace to the hearers" (Ephesians 4:29). Stop all corrupting speech before it leaves your mouth. Put forth a conscious effort to speak in a way that builds up and encourages others.

4. **Honor others with your speech.** "Honor all people. Love the brotherhood. Fear God. Honor the king" (1 Peter 2:17). We are to hold all people

(not just our rulers) in high esteem. This will impact the way we treat them and the attitude we have toward them, but it will also affect the way we talk to them and about them.

5. **Learn to live in God's presence.** God is always present (Psalm 139:7-10), which means He hears every word we say. David acknowledged this fact. "For there is not a word on my tongue, but behold, O Lord, You know it altogether" (v. 4). This is why Jesus said we will give an account for every idle word we speak. God hears every word! We need to learn to talk as if God is present for every conversation. "Let the words of my mouth and the meditation of my heart be acceptable in Your sight, O Lord, my strength and my Redeemer" (Psalm 19:14).

6. **Pray for God's help.** David prayed for God's help regarding his speech. "Set a guard, O Lord, over my mouth; keep watch over the door of my lips" (Psalm 141:3). When was the last time you asked God to help you with a bad habit? If you ask Him, God will help you overcome the sinful habit of using bad language.

7. **Keep your heart pure.** Your mouth speaks what is already in your heart. "Either make the tree good and its fruit good, or else make the tree bad and its fruit bad; for a tree is known by its fruit. Brood of vipers! How can you, being evil, speak good things? For out of the abundance of the heart the mouth speaks. A good man out of the good treasure of his heart brings forth good things, and an evil man out of the evil treasure brings forth evil things" (Matthew 12:33-35). We need to keep our hearts pure. We don't need to be listening to filthy language and dirty stories or watching sinful TV programs. If our hearts are pure, the fruit of our lips will be pure. "Keep your heart with all diligence, for out of it spring the issues of life. Put away from you a deceitful mouth, and put perverse lips far from you" (Proverbs 4:23-24).

Conclusion

On the night that Jesus was betrayed, Peter denied knowing Him, but those who stood by would not accept Peter's denial. They had convincing evidence to the contrary. "Surely you also are one of them, for your speech betrays you" (Matthew 26:73). Peter spoke like a Galilean. He could claim that he didn't know Jesus of Galilee, but his speech told them otherwise.

We can claim to be Christians, but when we speak like the world, we betray the fact that we are not true followers of Christ. "And do not be conformed to this world, but be transformed by the renewing of your mind, that you may prove what is that good and acceptable and perfect will of God" (Romans 12:2).

The use of corrupt words, filthy speech, profanity, and euphemisms is evidence of a shallow mind, lack of self-control, and lack of respect for others. The English language has over one million words with which we can express ourselves. Surely, we can communicate without cussing or using God's name in vain.

Questions

1. Explain why our words have the power to justify or condemn us (Matthew 12:34). _____
   _____
   _____

2. Ephesians 5:4 condemns foolish talking and coarse jesting. Is it wrong for Christians to tell any kind of jokes? _____
   _____

3. Under the Law of Moses, what was to happen to the person who blasphemed the Lord's name (Leviticus 24:16)? _____
   _____
   _____

4. What are some appropriate times and ways to use God's name? _____
   _____
   _____

5. Explain what a euphemism is. _____
   _____
   _____

6. Why is it wrong for Christians to use euphemisms? _____
   _____
   _____

7. What should we learn to do before we speak (Proverbs 15:28; James 1:19)? _____
   _____

8. What should we strive to accomplish with our speech (Ephesians 4:29)?
   _____
   _____

LESSON 11 Sinful Speech 91

9. Discuss how we can honor others with our speech (1 Peter 2:17). _____
   _____
   _____

10. What fact led David to be careful with his words (Psalm 139:7-10; 19:14)?
    _____
    _____
    _____

Hatred

When we think of worldliness, hatred is not one of the first subjects that comes to our minds. However, the attitudes and actions hatred produces are very much a part of the sinful things of the world. "For we ourselves were also once foolish, disobedient, deceived, serving various lusts and pleasures, living in malice and envy, hateful and hating one another" (Titus 3:3).

Hate's bitter fruits plague our world. Innocent people are made the victims of violence, pain, and sorrow, while those who hate are eventually ruined by their own poison. Unfortunately, Christians are sometimes troubled by sinful feelings of hatred.

Hatred defined

Hate is a feeling of strong antagonism and dislike; it is often accompanied by a desire to lash out and harm others.

In the Old Testament, the word hate is usually translated from the Hebrew word *sane*. This word "expresses an emotional attitude toward persons and things which are opposed, detested, despised, and with which one wishes to have no contact or relationship. Whereas love draws and unites, hate separates and keeps distant. The hated and hating persons are considered odious, utterly unappealing" (Van Groningen 880).

In the New Testament, the word hate is usually translated from the Greek word *miseo*, which refers to "malicious and unjustifiable feelings towards others, whether towards the innocent or by mutual animosity" (Vine 292). This is the way we most often use and understand the word hate.

> **Hatred** stirs up **strife**, but **love** covers all **sins**.
> - Proverbs 10:12

However, Vine also defines *miseo* (hate) as "a right feeling of aversion from what is evil." An aversion is the act of turning away from something we find to be repugnant. It is in this sense that God hates sin (Proverbs 6:16-19), Jesus hates sin (Revelation 2:6), and we learn to hate every false way (Psalm 119:104).

It is not always wrong for the child of God to hate. "To everything there is a season, a time for every purpose under heaven... A time to love, and a time to hate..." (Ecclesiastes 3:1, 8). It is wrong to have malicious and unjustifiable feelings of animosity toward people, but it is right for Christians to have and exercise deep feelings of aversion toward things that are evil in God's sight.

The bitter fruits of hatred

Just as a tree is known by its fruits (Matthew 12:33), sinful hatred is known by the fruits it produces.

1. **Stirs up trouble.** "Hatred stirs up strife, but love covers all sins" (Proverbs 10:12). While love seeks to cover sin to spare others from trouble and shame, hatred relishes the opportunity to expose the sins of others and bring them strife and shame. Hatred leads to violence. Hatred destroys lives, families, churches, and communities.

   Disciples of Christ are to be peacemakers, not troublemakers (Matthew 5:9). Paul said, "If it is possible, as much as depends on you, live peaceably with all men" (Romans 12:18). Sometimes, peace seems impossible because one person is intent upon causing another harm. However, if we entertain and harbor hatred in our own hearts, we do not contribute to peace among our fellowmen.

2. **Leads to murder.** Joseph's brothers hated him (Genesis 37:4, 5, 8). This hatred led to thoughts of murder (v. 20). Our legal system recognizes a difference between premeditated murder

> Blessed are the **peacemakers**, for they shall be called **sons of God**.
> - Matthew 5:9

and accidental death. So did the Law of Moses. Premeditated murder was (and still is) the result of hate. "But if anyone hates his neighbor, lies in wait for him, rises against him and strikes him mortally, so that he dies..." (Deuteronomy 19:11).

The person who hates is a murderer. "Whoever hates his brother is a murderer, and you know that no murderer has eternal life abiding in him" (1 John 3:15). This is a serious charge, but it is true. "This does not mean that he has committed the act of murder; or, that he is as guilty as if he had committed the act of murder; or, that God will hold him responsible for the act of murder. What is meant is, he has exhibited the disposition and spirit of a murderer; he has allowed passions to arise in his heart which, when carried to their ultimate ends, result in murder" (Woods 279).

Just as looking for the purpose of lusting is adultery in one's heart (Matthew 5:27-28), so also hatred toward another person is murder in one's heart. Both of these attitudes, if left unchecked and taken to their natural end, result in sin. However, because the Lord sees the heart (1 Samuel 16:7; 1 Peter 3:4), harboring lust or hatred in the heart is also sin. The heart of a murderer and the heart of one who hates his brother look the same to God.

3. **Produces wicked words.** While murder is an extreme and relatively rare act, we often express hatred through our words, and these words inflict harm. "A lying tongue hates those who are crushed by it, and a flattering mouth works ruin" (Proverbs 26:28).

Abrasive, abusive, rude speech comes from a heart filled with hate (Matthew 12:33-37). Gossip, slander, faultfinding, and false witnessing are the products of hate. We will answer for the words we spoke in anger. When we feel anger being aroused, we need to have the presence of mind to control our tongues (Ephesians 4:26-27).

> Whoever **hates** his brother is a **murderer**, and you know that no murderer has **eternal life** abiding in him.
>
> - 1 John 3:15

4. **Seeks revenge.** Unresolved hatred breeds resentment and fuels a desire for vengeance. It is only natural for us to strike back when we suffer wrong, but the Lord calls on us to love our enemies, to do good to those who hate us, to bless and pray for those who curse us, and to treat all men the way we want to be treated (Luke 6:27-31). Hatred does not allow us to follow this command.

5. **Destroys the soul.** While we may be tempted to dismiss hatred as nothing more than an undesirable emotion, we need to remember that Paul listed it as a work of the flesh (Galatians 5:19-21). Those who are given to hatred "will not inherit the kingdom of God." One who hates his brother is a murderer, and "no murderer has eternal life abiding in him" (1 John 3:15).

   When a bee stings, it injects its venom and inflicts pain on its victim, but then the bee dies. The same is true of those who hate. They cause others to suffer now, but they are the ones who will suffer eternal torment.

Overcoming hatred and the violence it causes

Hate is a real and powerful emotion. It exists for a reason. It is an unconscious reaction to lash out at what seems to be harming or diminishing us. We can't ignore hate or hope it will go away on its own. We must actively work at removing hatred from our hearts and lives.

1. **Let it go.** If hatred is the result of past injuries or experiences, we need to let go of those things (Philippians 3:13). Negative experiences become defining moments in our lives only if we choose to live in them and allow them to define who we are. Hatred is a strong emotion, and strong emotions are stirred by significant events. Pray that God will help you let go of those negative things (1 Peter 5:7).

2. **Resolve issues with others.** If you have feelings of hatred (antagonism, malice, ill will) towards others because of things they have done, go to them and seek to get it resolved (Matthew 18:15-17; 5:23-24). Allowing animosity to grow only makes it worse. The hatred stays in your heart; it poisons your mind; it bears its harmful fruits; and you will lose your soul. Remember that the person you hate is also made in the image of God. It is not fitting to entertain feelings of hatred towards that person (James 3:9).

3. **Overcome your pride.** We often feel hatred toward others because we feel we have been ignored, disrespected, or diminished by them. These problems arise because of pride. Wars and fights arise because people focus on themselves (James 4:1-3). We are not to focus only on our own

interests, but also on the interests of others (Philippians 2:3-4).

4. **Have regard for good things.** "Repay no one evil for evil. Have regard for good things in the sight of all men" (Romans 12:17). Stop looking for things to hate, and reasons to hate others. Learn to replace your desire for vengeance with a desire to do good. Seek to be thought of as one who does good and finds good in others, not one who looks for reasons to hate (1 Peter 3:9).

5. **Put God at the center of your life.** Man was created to have fellowship with God. When man removes God from His rightful place, he eventually becomes his own god. When this happens, love is replaced by pride, selfish desires, hatred, and violence.

   "And even as they did not like to retain God in their knowledge, God gave them over to a debased mind, to do those things which are not fitting; being filled with all unrighteousness, sexual immorality, wickedness, covetousness, maliciousness; full of envy, murder, strife, deceit, evil-mindedness; they are whisperers, backbiters, haters of God, violent, proud, boasters, inventors of evil things, disobedient to parents, undiscerning, untrustworthy, unloving, unforgiving, unmerciful" (Romans 1:28-31).

6. **Learn to love as God loves.** Love is the opposite of hate and is the solution to hatred (1 John 3:14-16). However, we must learn how to love as God loves, not as the world loves. "You have heard that it was said, 'You shall love your neighbor and hate your enemy.' But I say to you, love your enemies, bless those who curse you, do good to those who hate you, and pray for those who spitefully use you and persecute you, that you may be sons of your Father in heaven; for He makes His sun rise on the evil and on the good, and sends rain on the just and on the unjust" (Matthew 5:43-45).

> …not returning **evil** for evil or **reviling** for reviling, but on the contrary **blessing**…
>
> - 1 Peter 3:9

Hate is an emotion, but true love (*agape* love) is not an emotion. It is a command. We can love when the world prompts us to hate! We must learn how.

Conclusion

While it is true that Christians must hate sin and every evil way, such hate should not identify us. We are to be recognized by the world because of our love. "A new commandment I give to you, that you love one another; as I have loved you, that you also love one another. By this all will know that you are My disciples, if you have love for one another" (John 13:34-35).

Hate is an emotion, and sometimes it arises for legitimate reasons, but allowing it to remain in your heart is very dangerous. Given time and opportunity, hatred expresses itself in sinful ways, harms others, stops your light from shining in this dark world, hinders the cause of Christ, and eventually costs your soul.

Questions

1. Define the word hate. Do not cite modern sources or your personal feelings. Consult a dictionary and explain what the word really means.
   _____
   _____
   _____

2. Why is there a natural connection between hatred and violence?
   _____
   _____

3. Is it always wrong for a Christian to hate? Explain why or why not.
   _____
   _____
   _____

4. In what manner are we to live with others (Romans 12:18)? _____
   _____
   _____

5. What extreme act of violence is the natural result or product of hate (Deuteronomy 19:11)? _____

6. Explain why God calls the Christian who hates his brother "a murderer" (1 John 3:15). _____
   _____
   _____

7. Where do malicious and harmful words originate (Matthew 12:34-35)?
   _____
   _____

8. Where do wars and fights come from (James 4:1-6)?_____
   _____

9. To whom does vengeance belong (Romans 12:17-21)? _____

10. In what ways is the Christian to be identified?
    Matthew 5:9 _____
    John 13:34-35 _____
    2 Timothy 2:24-26 _____
    James 3:17_____
    1 Peter 3:9 _____

Lesson 13

A Bad Reputation

"A good name is to be chosen rather than great riches, loving favor rather than silver and gold" (Proverbs 22:1).

A person's reputation (good or bad) consists of other people's judgments of his overall qualities. It is the estimation in which a person is held by others. A good reputation is a very valuable thing. You may not think much about it, but God says to choose it over silver and gold.

A good reputation is one of the greatest prizes a person can possess. One with a good reputation is considered to be trustworthy. A good reputation cannot be purchased or demanded—only earned. It is not a right but a gift, offered on the basis of a lengthy history of reliable contributions to the lives of other people.

Jesus likened His disciples to salt and light (Matthew 5:13-16). Each of these substances has a powerful influence. Salt can preserve food, create thirst, melt ice, and enhance flavor. Light can give heat, dispel darkness, and enlighten man's awareness of his surroundings.

A good reputation equips God's children with influence and provides opportunities to do much good for the cause of Christ. Elders, deacons, and preachers must be men of good reputation (1 Timothy 3:7; Acts 6:3; 1 Timothy 4:12). However, God expects every Christian to take his reputation seriously and maintain his good influence.

Jesus warned that salt can lose its flavor and actually become harmful. "Salt is good; but if the salt has lost its flavor, how shall it be seasoned?

> You are the **light** of the **world**. A city that is set on a hill cannot be **hidden**.
>
> - Matthew 5:14

It is neither fit for the land nor for the dunghill, but men throw it out. He who has ears to hear, let him hear!" (Luke 14:34-35). This defiled salt may have lost its positive influence, but it is still harmful to vegetation. It cannot be thrown out on the ground, or even disposed of in a pile of manure (fertilizer). The ruined salt must be discarded into the street where vegetation is not wanted.

Nehemiah was doing a very important work for God. His enemies opposed this work, but Nehemiah rose above their opposition. On one occasion, they tried to destroy his reputation (Nehemiah 6:10-13). They told him his life was in danger and advised him to flee into the temple for safety. Nehemiah realized what they were doing and refused to participate. He carefully protected his reputation so the work could continue.

Why are God's servants careful to protect their reputation? Because they realize there is something more important to consider than themselves. Representing God and effectively doing His work are the most important considerations. Every Christian is a walking, talking, 24-hour advertisement for the Lord, the gospel, and the local church. What kind of messages are we sending to the world?

Let's consider some areas in which we must protect our reputations.

Our actions

God expects His people to behave appropriately. To protect one's reputation and influence, it is important to avoid some activities.

We must depart from iniquity (2 Timothy 2:19) and abstain from every form of evil (1 Thessalonians 5:21-22). We are not allowed to enjoy the sinful pleasures of the world (1 Peter 4:1-4). We cannot be involved in such things as fornication, dancing, or mixed swimming. We cannot drink alcohol or use drugs and tobacco. Even if we are abstaining, we do not need to be present at drinking parties or places where others are using and abusing drugs and alcohol. Our presence lends our endorsement, and thus weakens our influence against these sins.

"Beloved, I beg you as sojourners and pilgrims, abstain from fleshly lusts which war against the soul, having your conduct honorable among the Gentiles, that when they speak against you as evildoers, they may, by your good works which they observe, glorify God in the day of visitation" (1 Peter 2:11-12). Honorable conduct among unbelievers is more important that enjoying the passing pleasures of sin (Hebrews 11:25). A moment of weakness can ruin one's credibility with the lost and hinder his chances of influencing them to follow Christ.

Our words

Watching your speech is a very important part of maintaining your reputation. Words reveal what is really in the heart. "Brood of vipers! How can you, being evil, speak good things? For out of the abundance of the heart the mouth speaks. A good man out of the good treasure of his heart brings forth good things, and an evil man out of the evil treasure brings forth evil things" (Matthew 12:34-35).

The importance of maintaining godly speech is exhibited in the fact that people expect Christians to talk in a certain manner. It is unnatural for a spring to produce different kinds of water, or for a fruit tree to produce different kinds of fruit (James 3:9-12). It will be difficult to convince people that you are a citizen of Heaven when you talk like a person of the world (Matthew 26:73). How can you promote the word of truth when you tell lies (Ephesians 4:25)? How can you impart grace to others when your mouth produces corrupt words and foul language (Ephesians 4:29)? How can you encourage people to be saved from this perverse generation when your speech is filled with perverse stories and dirty jokes (Ephesians 5:3-4)?

> Out of the **same mouth** proceed **blessing** and **cursing**. My brethren, these things ought **not** to be so.
>
> - James 3:10

Our companions

This is an area where Christians have a real challenge. Like Israel of old, we must remain separate from the sinful world around us. "Come out from among them and be separate, says the Lord. Do not touch what is unclean, and I will receive you" (2 Corinthians 6:17). At the same time, we are expected to exert a positive influence on the world around us. We are the salt of the earth, but salt must contact a substance before it can influence that substance. How do we influence the people of the world without allowing them to influence us?

We are allowed to associate with worldly people (1 Corinthians 5:9-12). We may mix socially and may

> And have **no fellowship** with the unfruitful works of **darkness**, but rather **expose** them.
>
> - Ephesians 5:11

even have dealings with sinful and wicked people. Jesus ate with sinners to teach and influence them (Mark 2:15-17). However, we must never fellowship their evil practices (Ephesians 5:11).

There is a difference between associating with worldly people and preferring their company. The Bible warns of the corrupting danger of bad influences. "Do not be deceived: 'Bad company corrupts good morals'" (1 Corinthians 15:33, NASB). Do not deceive yourself into thinking you are an exception to this rule. Evil influences corrupt good habits, manners, and morals. Walking with the ungodly leads to standing with sinners and sitting with scoffers (Psalm 1:1).

Solomon warned, "He who walks with wise men will be wise, but the companion of fools will be destroyed" (Proverbs 13:20). We tend to take on the characteristics of our close associates. If we choose to walk with fools, we will learn their lifestyles, standards, and attitudes. These will prove to be hard habits to break. The Lord would have us save ourselves from this burden by avoiding evil companions.

Involvement in social media

Most Christians have an online presence that includes participating in social media. Social media has advantages and benefits, but it is also full of dangers.

It is alarming how many Christians post and "like" ungodly things on social media. Posts are filled with pictures of immodest dress, young people attending dances, drinking alcohol, and so on. Christians recommend TV programs and movies filled with bad language and sinful content. Some Christians have even shared religious posts that contained false doctrine.

Social media allows us to look into the hearts of our brethren, and what we see is sometimes disappointing. When confronted about such posts, some Christians try to turn the tables and blame their brethren for looking at their posts and judging their hearts. This is unfortunate. Remember, we are talking about our reputations. The people of the world recognize that input on social media expresses one's reputation.

> "More than half of employers (57 percent) that check job candidates' social media say they've seen content that has caused them to eliminate a person as a job contender... The top three turnoffs are provocative or inappropriate content (40 percent), posts about drinking or using drugs (36 percent), and discriminatory comments (31 percent)... And based on the survey, the scrutiny continues after you're hired: 48 percent of respondents say they monitor current employees' social media activity" (https://www.cnbc.com/2018/08/10/digital-dirt-may-nix-that-job-you-were-counting-on-getting.html).

Social media can be an effective tool for furthering the gospel in a digital age. However, it can also become a Christian's means of damaging his reputation and ruining his credibility for the cause of Christ.

Conclusion

God has given us great potential with our personal reputations. Each of us has a unique influence circle (the people we know and can influence for good). God will hold us responsible for the ways we have used our influence.

Your reputation is a fragile thing, and you must protect it with diligence. The person who claims to be a Christian and yet lives like the sinners in the world is a hypocrite. Such a person destroys his influence and reputation. Always remember what the Lord taught about the salt losing its flavor.

> "Salt is good; but if the salt has lost its flavor, how shall it be seasoned? It is neither fit for the land nor for the dunghill, but men throw it out. He who has ears to hear, let him hear!" (Luke 14:34-35).

Questions

1. What is a reputation? _____
   _____
   _____

2. What value does God place on your reputation (Proverbs 22:1)? _____
   _____
   _____

3. What is influence? _____
   _____
   _____

4. Explain why elders, deacons, and preachers must be men of good reputation (Acts 6:3; 1 Timothy 3:7; 4:12). _____
   _____
   _____

5. Explain what happens to the Christian who loses his good reputation (Luke 14:34-35). _____
   _____
   _____

6. What conduct must we maintain before unbelievers (1 Peter 2:12)?
   _____
   _____

7. What role does your speech play in maintaining your reputation (Matthew 12:33-35; James 3:9-12)? _____
   _____
   _____

8. What does bad company do (1 Corinthians 15:33)? _____
   _____

9. Why did Jesus eat with sinners (Mark 2:15-17)? _____
   _____
   _____

10. Paul said that he became all things to all men that he might save some (1 Corinthians 9:19-23). Does this give us the right to join worldly people in sinful activities? Explain why or why not. _____
    _____
    _____
    _____

11. Explain how a misuse of social media can damage your reputation.
    _____
    _____
    _____

12. How is a Christian to remain separate from the world (2 Corinthians 6:17) and still be the salt of the earth (Matthew 5:13?) _____
_____
_____
_____

Bibliography

Blackaby, Randy. *Blessed To Bless.* Bowling Green, KY, One Stone Press, 2013. Print.

Caldwell, C. G. "Colly". *Truth Commentaries, The Gospel According to Luke.* Bowling Green, Kentucky: Guardian of Truth Foundation, 2011. Print.

Dana, H. E. *The New Testament World.* Nashville, Tennessee: Broadman Press, 1937. Print.

Demarest, Gary. *Mastering the Old Testament, Volume 3: Leviticus.* Dallas, Texas: Word Publishing, 1990. Print.

Grasham, William W. Ph.D. *Truth For Today Commentary, Genesis 1-22.* Searcy, AR, Resource Publications, 2014. Print.

Guralnik, David B., Editor in Chief. *Webster's New World Dictionary of the American Language, Second College Edition,* New York, NY, Prentice Hall Press, 1986. Print.

Hamilton, Clinton D. *Truth Commentaries, 1 Peter.* Bowling Green, Kentucky: Guardian of Truth Foundation, 1995. Print.

Harris, R. Laird, Gleason L. Archer, Jr., and Bruce K. Waltke. *Theological Wordbook of the Old Testament.* Chicago: Moody Press, 1980. Print

MacArthur, John F. *The MacArthur New Testament Commentary, 1 Corinthians.* Chicago, IL: Moody Publishers, 1984. Print.

Miller, Dave. Ph.D. *Sexual Anarchy.* Montgomery, Alabama: Apologetics Press, 2006. Print.

Morris, Leon. *The First and Second Epistles to the Thessalonians.* Grand Rapids, Michigan: Wm. B. Eerdmans Publishing, 1959. Print.

Pollard, Jeff. *Christian Modesty and the Public Undressing of America.* San Antonio, Texas: The Vision Forum, Inc. 2004. Print.

Roper, David L. *Truth For Today Commentary, 1 & 2 Timothy and Titus.* Searcy, AR, Resource Publications, 2017. Print.

Thayer, Joseph H. *Thayer's Greek-English Lexicon of the New Testament.* Peabody, MA: Hendrickson Publishers, 1996. Print.

Vine, W.E., Merrill F. Unger, and William White, Jr. *Vine's Complete Expository Dictionary of Old and New Testament Words,* Nashville, Thomas Nelson Inc., 1985. print.

Wenham, Gordon J. *World Biblical Commentary, Genesis 1-15*. Waco, Texas: Word Books, 1987. Print.

Woods, Guy N. *A Commentary on the New Testament Epistles of Peter, John, and Jude.* Nashville, Tennessee: Gospel Advocate Company, 1955. Print.

www.ingramcontent.com/pod-product-compliance
Lightning Source LLC
Chambersburg PA
CBHW070620050426
42450CB00011B/3093